The Lace
HERITAGE

by
DAVID LOWE
and
JACK RICHARDS

Copyright © D. E. Lowe, J. E. Richards, 1984.

All rights reserved. No part of this work may be reproduced or used in any form without written permission.

Published by Nottingham Lace Centre Limited, Severns Building, Castle Road, Nottingham.

The City of Lace by David Lowe and Jack Richards, published 1982 and re-printed 1983, is available from the Lace Centre at the above address.

To
Mavis
and
Marjorie

Acknowledgements

The authors would like to express their appreciation to the many people who made this book possible. We are indebted to Councillor Mrs Ivy Matthews, Deputy Lord Mayor of Nottingham, 1983-4, for kindly providing the personal message which appears on the back cover and Miss Christina Foyle, who wrote the foreword and gave us great encouragement. We are proud and honoured that these two special ladies should wish to associate their names with this publication. Our wives, Mavis and Marjorie, showed commendable forbearance, read proofs and gave marvellous support in the hectic time before going to press.

Several individuals gave considerable help with certain chapters. We are extremely grateful to Ron Leavers who kindly allowed us to examine family papers relating to his famous ancestor and the assistance given by staff of the Nottinghamshire Record Office.

Chapter Two (Thomas Adams and his Empire) and Chapter Eight (Lace Market Revival) owe much to Geoffrey Oldfield, a member of the council of the Thoroton Society. We drew heavily on his papers, built up during years of assiduous research. We are also grateful for the information about the industrial building survey, supplied by Stuart Warburton. Special thanks go to local bobbin lace teacher Ann Seals for her help with Chapter Nine (New Trends, Old Trends) and we are extremely grateful to David Attenborough and Barry Stocks of the Birkin Group for giving so generously of their time to enable Chapter Ten (Lace in the Computer Age) to be written.

Several local authority departments gave splendid co-operation, notably the city's Planning and Public Relations Departments. Photographs and illustrations came from many sources. Invaluable assistance in our researches was given by the Nottingham Evening Post Library; the Nottinghamshire Local Studies Library; Mr David Griggs, of the Lace Research Association; lace firms and interested individuals.

During the various production stages, we were fortunate to be able to call on the combined experience of Peter Mould, Colin Simpson, Tony Moss, David Butler, Barry Hemmings and several others. We are also grateful to John Richards of Workshop Design, who designed the cover and helped with the lay-out, and Jim Bancroft, who took the cover photograph.

Finally a word of appreciation to the Directors of Nottingham Lace Centre Ltd., who backed the publication and gave the authors a free hand in compiling The Lace Heritage.

Bibliography Contents

Many sources have been used in The Lace Heritage. This select bibliography gratefully acknowledges the following works:

Birkin Group, 1962-82: printed by J. M. Tatler and Son Ltd., Derby.

Emrys Bryson: Portrait of Nottingham (Robert Hale).

Stanley D. Chapman: The Early Factory Masters (David and Charles).

W. Dearden: History, Topography and Directory of the Town of Nottingham (Nottingham 1834).

William Felkin: A History of the Machine Wrought Hosiery and Lace Manufacturers (1867 reprinted 1967 with an introduction by Dr S. D. Chapman.

Richard Iliffe and Wilfred Baguley: Volumes of Victorian Nottingham (Nottingham Historical Film Unit) and Old Nottingham, The Streets and Workplaces of the Lace Market (Evening Post Publication).

Rev W. Milton: Religion and Business — Memorials of Thomas Adams JP of Nottingham, Lace Merchant (London 1874).

Nottingham City Planning Department: A Conservation Policy for the Lace Market 1974; Lace Market Improvement Areas and Europa Nostra Awards, 1983.

Geoffrey Oldfield: Nottingham's Lace Market (Textile History, 1984).

Foreword by CHRISTINA FOYLE

From the Director's Office

W. & G. FOYLE LTD.
Booksellers
119-125, CHARING CROSS ROAD,
LONDON, W. C. 2.
(Registered Office)

Directors:
CHRISTINA FOYLE
RONALD BATTY
Registered No.
945131 ENGLAND

Telephone:
01-437 5660
Telegrams:
POYLIBRA, LONDON W.C.2.

Your Ref

Our Ref

"The Lace Heritage" is a book that will appeal to lovers of beauty, of travel and adventure and to everyone interested in the inspiring tale of British skill and ingenuity.

David Lowe and Jack Richards tell a wonderful story; but for me the charm of the book is that it is about lace. Beautiful lace - whether adorning a woman, a church, or the home, is one of the really lovely things, like flowers, the spring, sunsets and poetry, that embellish our earth, and may this book, that tells us so much about it, have the great success it deserves.

Christina Foyle

V

vi

Contents

Foreword by Christina Foyle.
Preface.
Chapter One — Our family links with John Leavers.
Chapter Two — Thomas Adams and his Empire.
Chapter Three — Early Days by Jack Richards.
Chapter Four — More Adventures of a Lace Exporter.
(i) New Zealand;
(ii) Australia
(iii) Fiji and Honolulu.

Chapter Five — Cowcatchers and All!
(i) San Francisco
(ii) South Africa.

Chapter Six — Life on the Ocean Waves.
(i) Near Miss
(ii) Cruising.

Chapter Seven — After St Mary's Place.
(i) Lace in Europe
(ii)The Lace Centre.

Chapter Eight — Lace Market Revival.
Chapter Nine — New Trends, Old Trends.
Chapter Ten — Lace in the Computer Age.
Picture Credits.
Lace Collections.

vii

viii

Preface

Friends suggested we write *The City of Lace* while there was still a tale to tell. The book, much to our delight, has reached 15 countries to date, reminding us that lace has international appeal.

We received letters from far and wide, particularly Europe, the United States and Australia. Co-author Jack Richards realised he had many adventures from his overseas trips still to recount and we also wanted to publish more of the photographs of people and places offered from several sources. So this follow-up book, *The Lace Heritage,* is the result.

It appears in an auspicious year. For 1984 is the 700th anniversary of Nottingham being granted a Charter by Edward 1. This empowered the Burgesses of Nottingham to elect a mayor for the town and a bailiff for each of the two burghs. The mayor was to be elected in the Feast of St Michael; so it is assumed that the first Mayor was elected on September 29, 1284.

Mayors continued to be elected annually until 1928 when, on July 30 of that year, King George announced that, in consideration of the antiquities and importance of the city "from this time forward the Chief Magistrate of the city shall bear the style and title of Lord Mayor of Nottingham." The first holder was the then Mayor, Ald Edmund Huntsman.

The Charter also empowered the holding of a 15-day fair. This was in addition to the September fair — later to become the world-famous Nottingham Goose Fair — opened on the first Thursday of October by the Lord Mayor ringing a set of traditional bells. In modern times the three-day spectacle draws half a million revellers to the Forest site.

In recent years the city has made rapid strides as the centre of an expanding tourist industry, which brings £350m a year to the region and employs 30,000 people in Nottingham.

Mr Jeff Hamblin, Director of the East Midlands Tourist Board, told top executives: "We all have to be aware that Nottingham and the county have something to offer and we must do our utmost to shout about it."

Heeding those words the lace and textile industry is making a big effort to promote itself.

The Lace Centre opened in 1980 as a unique co-operative venture, involving eight leading lace firms. It now attracts 100,000 visitors a year to the Severn's Building, 15th century premises near Nottingham Castle, generously made available by the City Council.

Other exiting projects such as the Textile Centre are underway while the Lace Market Centre will provide facilities under one roof for businesses to hold small conferences, meetings and commercial exhibitions, together with tourist facilities and exhibitions for the general public.

The High Pavement Chapel will be an ideal "showcase" for Nottingham and its commerce and industry. A product of Victorian enterprise, its congregation held a virtual monopoly of Nottingham political life in the 18th and 19th centuries when at least 66 mayors were chapel members

It stands impressively only a stride away from Hollowstone, Nottingham's most ancient street. Here the original Anglo-Saxon tribe of Snot settled. They carved homes out of the soft sandstone and their 39 acre settlement became known as Snottingham.

When the Normans arrived they had difficulty pronouncing "Sn." So Nottingham was born. Now nine centuries or so later what better place to show how Nottingham has developed from settlement to city, display Lace Market history and promote city industry and commerce.

The City Council's sustained and imaginative conservation strategy has already paid off. More than £3m has been spent cleaning and restoring buildings in the area, introducing new housing and encouraging new businesses to the district.

This enterprising exercise in urban renewal — in the 50s and 60s it was a sadly rundown and neglected area — earned European recognition in 1983 when three city schemes shared a prestigious Europa Nostra Diploma of Merit.

So the future looks bright. While some sections of the lace industry are moving into the computer age, traditional skills, handed down through generations of lacemakers, remain very much alive. The trade also abounds with characters, some retired, some still hard at work.

Eighty-year-old Charles Lawson, Britain's oldest salesman, gets up at the crack of dawn to carry on his job as agent for a Nottingham lace firm. He has no intention of retiring.

We have also discovered a man directly related to John Leavers,the Nottinghamshire framesmith whose invention founded the lace industry.

So you see, the lace heritage is as rich as ever . . .

CHAPTER ONE

Our Family Links with John Leavers

Ron Leavers of Ravenshead, near Nottingham, has a famous great-great grandfather . . . John Leavers, founder of the modern lace industry.

Deposited at Nottinghamshire Record Office is a collection of family papers which give a fascinating insight into a slice of 18th century life.

Leavers was a complex character. He was born at Sutton-in-Ashfield in 1786 and learned his trade as a "setter up" of lace machines in Radford. It was during the stormy days of Luddism and frame smashing that he practically isolated himself for two years in a Nottingham garret, near Canning Circus. Here in 1813 he built a prototype of the machine, which make the world-famous laces bearing his name today.

His improved machine, first used in a factory belonging to Stevenson and Skipworth in St James's Street, was of enormous value to the lace trade.

Decades later textile historian William Felkin estimated that Leavers lace was contributing £3m out of a total trade turnover of £5m.

Yet, during his life, John Leavers frequently did not have a shilling in his pocket. Disillusioned, he left for France in 1821 with his brothers Thomas and Joseph, and they built lace machines at Grand Courenne, a suburb of Rouen. These machines formed the basis of the Calais lace industry.

John's first wife, Anne, who came from Heanor, Derbyshire, died in 1824, aged 40. It appears the couple were childless.

John remarried and his second wife, Francoise Massiotty, was a native of Brussels. They had two sons and two daughters.

The eldest son, William, was born in 1826 and followed in his father's footsteps as a framesmith but later became a card manufacturer.

Edward, the second son born in 1829, seems to have been the rebel of the family. Sometime in 1840 he returned to England and built lace machines in the Nottingham area and later in London. He was a skilled musician, a talent undoubtedly inherited from his father, who was bandmaster to the National Guard and an accomplished French horn player.

One of the most interesting letters to survive is the one John Leavers wrote from Rouen to Edward in 1848. Dated March 17, it reads:

1

1: John Leavers built his famous lace machine in the garret of this house (demolished 1959) in St Helen's Street, Canning Circus.

Dear Edward,
"We have a great ceremony here next Sunday with the Mayor and all the authorities and National Guard to proclaim the Republic. I have sent you five tickets and beg you will see Jack tonight and get him to deliver them directly so as nobody will miss coming as I expect all the village being present.
"You may ask your Uncle Joseph to come. If he can't come you might try his coat and chaqueot; if it fits you borrow it for Sunday."
John Leavers died six months later on September 24, 1848, aged 62. Though he was buried with military honours, few details are recorded of his death. French newspapers of the day, one assumes, were too busy covering the Revolution.

Two buildings flanking a courtyard, where Leavers did much of his machine building, still stand in Grand Courenne, next to the church on the main road. There is also a street in the village named after the inventor. At the time of his death he also owned a piece of ploughing land and at least two other properties, one of which has been demolished. Edward, living in Nottingham, authorised William, jointly with his mother and sister Sarah, to mortgage the house and workshop for up to 2,000 francs.

One letter from John's widow to Edward, dated November 25, 1851, reveals some resentment towards France because William was not allowed a vote "as the son of a foreigner." She reflects: "We have some work but not so much as we want. But you have to be contented." She also mentions that William would be pleased if Edward sent him an English newspaper.

Another letter from 1852 suggests Edward felt he was being badly treated by his master. She says William has plenty of work but little ribbon for his card-manufacturing trade.

She also mentions the visit of an inventor from Paris to see a jacquard. "But I think he's stuck in the mud with his machine. He wants a good English machine," she writes.

Occasionally she refers to her failing health. In one letter, she complains of pain in her right leg and says her head is "full of lumps." John Leavers' widow died on January 4, 1859.

But what happened to the children? Little is known about the descendants of William, Fanny and Sarah. John Leavers' younger brother Thomas married Elizabeth Sallis at Grand Courenne in 1824. They had no children.

On the other hand his other brother Joseph had a large family, four sons and two daughters, some of whom are thought to have returned to the Nottingham area. But so far it has not been possible to trace the descendants beyond the first generation. But it is known that Edward married Fanny Wynn and they had a son Arthur, born in 1853.

Arthur had two sons, Harold, born in 1887 and Horace Arthur, born in 1889 as well as four daughters, all of whom married and had children. They were all good musicians.

Harold, who died in 1956, had no children. But Horace, who was killed in a road accident in March, 1943 had one child, a son, Ronald Arthur. He moved to London when he was 12 and the lace link was kept alive only by the stories he heard at his grandfather's knee.

It's a fascinating family tree. And it's good to know that the direct line from John Leavers, through Edward, Arthur, Horace Arthur and Ronald Arthur, will continue. For Ron has a son, Timothy Arthur.

As Ron reflects: "Why none of us thought to stick 'John' in somewhere I don't know. I'm afraid it seems to point to a certain lack of regard for our distinguished ancestor."

In fact it is a great source of pride whenever he travels to Nottingham for Ron to see the little plaque at Canning Circus, marking John Leavers' house, where the story started . . .

2: The Leavers plaque at Canning Circus.

3: Mr Ron Leavers.

CHAPTER TWO

Thomas Adams and his Empire

The lace trade was noted for penny pinching, secrecy and keen rivalry. And the age of intrigue was never more apparent than in 1823 when the expiry of Heathcoat's patent produced a frantic period known as twist net fever. Wages rose overnight. Farm labourers gave up the plough to try their luck at lacemaking and smiths and mechanics poured into Nottingham from Sheffield, Birmingham and Manchester. Two men working five-hour shifts, alternately, a total of 20 hours, could earn £5 a week, princely pay for those times.

Technically Heathcoat and Leavers determined the shape of future development. Though lace machines continued to be modified, enlarged and speeded up, the great age of contrivers and innovators was effectively over and there was now far less chance of mechanics rising from craftsmen to masters overnight.

Leavers machines, bigger, heavier and far more costly than the stocking frame, required a large building. So factories sprang up to replace the traditional workshop and cottage-based craft.

Though the boom soon subsided, the industry was now firmly established in Nottingham with Dearden's Directory of 1834 describing the many different sections of the trade — manufacturers, merchants, dealers, dressers, gassers, thread preparers and warpers.

It was soon found that children, some as young as five or six years old, could be easily trained to do many of the simpler tasks. Above all, they were cheap labour and could be employed for extremely long hours with virtually no laws to protect them. The Commissioners' Reports of 1843 and 1861 did much to bring the stark facts to light and led eventually to gradual improvements in working conditions.

Bad as the factory system was, it rarely touched the depths reached by domestic workshops in Nottingham. Dr William Watts, a resident medical officer, told the Commission he had seen packs of children, crowded into a small room.

"In lace drawing, the hours are commonly from 8am till later than 8pm. In lace running and mending, the hours are longer. I have often been told that the wages of a person of 22 or 23 are not more than 6d a day, working from 6am till 11pm with only intervals for meals. These are often taken without workers leaving the frame."

For women workers the conditions and long hours often produced curvature of the spine, TB, anaemia, difficult childbirth and a tendency to miscarry.

"Infants are often given laudanum in some form or other. This is frequently given pure after Godfrey's Cordial — a mixture of treacle and dissolved opium — has been given for some time.

"It is common among lace runners for a mother to support her infant on her lap, and to keep it quiet by the above means, so as to prevent her being disturbed at work. I have no doubt that many infants are destroyed by this system."

Surgeon Booth Eddison reported: "The whole class of lace workers becomes after a time permanently short-sighted. The condition is indicated by a particular prominence of the cornea. I am quite satisfied this is a consequence of beginning work at a very early age, six, seven and eight, when the eye is still growing."

The Archdeacon, the Ven George Wilkins, was sorely troubled by "much immorality" among the children of the Industrial Revolution. "The police say there has never been so greater a number of prostitutes. Of these, by far the most troublesome and the most abandoned are the younger ones. This immorality starts between boys and girls who associate together after they leave the factory. Girls then endeavour to turn their licentiousness into gain by prostitution. Girls are able to support themselves from their earnings in the needle trade. Indeed it is common to find parents, fathers in particular, who not only do little or nothing towards maintaining their family but live idly upon their children's earnings."

The remedy, he maintained, was education. "But how is this to prevail when in every street there are rooms full of children who are kept continually at the needle until late hours?" He said children of the poor, aged up to nine, should be educated a certain number of hours every day. Beyond that age, no child should be employed after 8pm.

In his 1844 report, J. R. Martin said sanitary conditions in some parts of Nottingham ranked among the worst in England. Refuse piled up in courts and alleys until it was sold for a few shillings and carted away by "muck majors." Cholera was still the terrible scourge and the average life span in some districts was 14 or 15 years — the worst figures "within the British empire."

More than 40,000 people were employed in the manufacture of cotton and silk stockings, lace and bobbin net. "The work is carried on in rooms usually overcrowded and ill-ventilated. It is common to find 15 to 20 children in a low garret, 12 ft square, working for 15 hours a day," reported Mr Martin.

An article in The Penny Magazine in March, 1843, described the lamentable lot of lace runners. "Little do those who see Nottingham's beautiful veils and capes in the attractive shop windows of London

6

imagine how many aching fingers and eyes, and perhaps hearts, have been concerned in their production."

Lace runners often earned only a halfpenny an hour. Most of the profits went to middle women, who collected work from manufacturers and charged the lace runners rent for using their wretched rooms.

Gradually the consciences of a few humane men were awakened. Such a man was Thomas Adams, an enlightened employer whose model lace warehouse in Stoney Street still stands. Adams was born at Worksop, Nottinghamshire in 1807, the son of a maltster. His father died while he was still a child and young Thomas was apprenticed to a Newark draper for seven years before he moved to London. There he met a young man who tricked him into going to France and dispossessed him of his money. Abandoned in Paris, he sought help from a lace manufacturer in England, eventually returning to London, where he worked in the warehouse of Bodens, a Derby-based lace firm and former partners of John Heathcoat.

Adams came to Nottingham in 1830 to start his own business, buying lace from the 1,200 or so makers of plain and decorated nets in the town and distributing the fabrics to wholesalers and retailers. In the same year he married Lucy Cullen, daughter of a Nottingham businessmen, at St Mary's Church.

Two years later he began a long partnership with James Page, a fellow Anglican and Tory, and a small number of manufacturers, to form Adams, Page and Co. The major impetus to Adams' business came after 1839 when the railway line from London to Nottingham was completed.

Wholesalers and exporters now flocked to Nottingham to buy their own nets and laces, whose quality and design had improved steadily over the previous 30 years. Adams seems to have concentrated on the home market but a connection with a London merchant bank suggests he may also have been selling in the Mediterranean. He hit a financial crisis in 1843-4 through the failure of an agent but soon recovered.

The years following the Nottingham Enclosure Act (1845) saw the old commercial heart of the town rebuilt as the Lace Market. Adams was expanding rapidly and in 1855 he proudly opened his palatial new warehouse, which soon employed 600 people, 500 of them women.

At that time most industrial premises in England were designed by engineers rather than architects. The building created by T. C. Hine — who with the exception of Watson Fothergill was surely the most ingenious and imaginative architect ever to stamp his mark on Nottingham — was so magnificent it was criticised for being too good.

The Nottingham Review devoted an entire page of small, tightly packed print, to describe the building and the opening ceremony. The five-storey structure was in the form of an E, its two wings flanking an imposing entrance. A handsome flight of stairs from the entrance hall led to a 13ft high salesroom lit by an immense central window. For workers of the time the accommodation was idyllic. They had spacious, well-lit rooms, a library, a classroom, a separate tea room for the men, washing facilities and a workers' dining room. There were even separate staircases

4: Portrait of Thomas Adams, which hung in the basement chapel of Adams warehouse.

for men and women workers while a heating apparatus, designed by London engineer Alfred Penny, circulated warm air around the building.

But most remarkable of all was the basement chapel, for which Adams appointed a chaplain, the Rev Edward Davies, to conduct services at precisely five minutes past eight each morning before work began. Adams prayed with his workers. He felt the 30-minute services, taken in company time, would "seek the blessing of God on our labours."

He also spoke of his desire to combine Christian principles with business. His own office was hung with inspirational biblical passages, including "what shall it profit a man if he shall gain the whole world and lose his own soul."

Employees and guests were entertained to a slap-up, opening day tea and afterwards there were more speeches, a brass band played and Mr White of the General Hospital exhibited his magic lantern. One speaker told the assembly: "I believe we are seeing a day dawn when there will be great anxiety within the lace trade generally to see the hours of labour reduced." He favoured a 2pm finish on Saturday afternoon to give workers proper time to prepare for the Sabbath.

The 1861 inquiry, in fact, succeeded in subjecting lace manufacturers to the Factory Act but the legislation did not extend to lace dressing and finishing houses. Thomas Adams thought the working day for children should end at 7pm — to give them time to attend evening school.

As well as giving substantial sums to found schools, he was also a great benefactor of churches, buying plots of likely land where he thought churches would be required as Nottingham grew. St Phillips' Church in Pennyfoot Street was designed as a "Thomas Adams Memorial Church" and there are stained glass windows in his memory in St Mary's Church and Lenton Church.

Adams emerged as the leading evangelical layman of his day. Elected to Nottingham Corporation in 1836, he was also a member of the Poor Law Board for many years but seldom attended and rarely spoke. "I can make money," he admitted. "But I cannot make a speech." And as a Tory, the Whig majority on the Corporation denied him the opportunity of becoming an Alderman or Mayor. So his main endeavour continued to be focussed on the welfare of his workers.

In 1865 Adams and Page became known as Thomas Adams and Company Ltd after incorporating under the Companies Act of 1862. The memorandum and articles of association, deposited at Nottinghamshire Record Office, contain two paragraphs not usually found in such documents. One of the objects of the company was set out as "establishing, managing and assisting churches, chapels, schools, libraries, banks, dispensaries, infirmaries, provident societies, clubs and other institutions for the benefit of persons employed by the company and their families and others."

One of the articles of association provided that the company shall always employ a chaplain of the Established Church to conduct services in the chapel at a salary of not less than £250 a year.

Thomas Adams himself was the principal subscriber of the first regis-

5: Adams warehouse, Stoney Street.

6: Adams chapel.

7: T. C. Hine's initials carved on the Birkin building in Broadway beside the instruments of his work.

tered company, having 6,650 shares out of the total of 11,200 issued. Two of his sons, Samuel and John, held a further 2,350 shares. Arthur Wells, a Nottingham solicitor, held 1,000 shares and three other lace merchants, Edward Massey, Frederick Mundy and Henry Price, between them held the balance of 1,200. All these, plus Clement Boughton Kingdon, of Hulland Hall, Derbyshire, were the first directors.

The foundation capital was £112,000 and the valuation of the property taken over by the company from the former partnership was £132,803. According to Adams' biographer, the Rev W. Milton, the shares paid 15% dividend and appreciated in value.

Adams, who had ten children, planned for Samuel and John to succeed him in the business. Sadly both died young. Soon after Samuel's death in 1870, Adams' own health broke down and he died in 1873, leaving an estate valued at £90,000.

Meanwhile the momentum of the main business was maintained for another two generations largely through Adams' policy of promoting senior clerks to the board of his company.

Frederick Carver, a man of uncompromising views on trade unions and women workers, took a leading role in Thomas Adams and Co Ltd, being a director by 1883 and later chairman until 1916.

In 1904, following a company reconstruction, the firm's name changed to Thomas Adams Ltd. The minute book of the first meeting of the board of the new company on July 15, 1904, has survived, together with two subsequent volumes, giving 40 years of the company's proceedings.

Nottingham lace was approaching the crest of a wave with Thomas Adams the trade's leading firm. Exports flourished and the company's 1914 handbook proudly proclaims: "The centre of the company is in Stoney Street and St Mary's Gate, large and commodious premises containing 14 departments where all classes of lace and net are prepared and despatched to every part of the world.

"The business relations of the company extend practically throughout the world, principally by sending out its own travellers to different countries. Some of them have to carry a collection containing more than 250,000 samples."

The company, along with Birkins and other firms, was visited by King George V and Queen Mary on June 24, 1914. A souvenir booklet contains photographs and a description of the firm, which even made its own soap and had its own deep wells supplying 1,000 gallons of water an hour. Over 2,000 were employed. The 1,400 employees at Stoney Street were mainly women, making up ladies wear — fancy neckwear, ruffles, pinafores, skirts, ruchings, blouses and bridal veils.

The outbreak of war shortly after the Royal visit had a marked effect on British trade and lace exports were particularly hard hit. As early as August 28, 1914, the board of Thomas Adams Ltd were informed that debts in South America were over £134,000 with nearly £72,000 overdue because of currency and international trade settlement problems.

Overseas trade did continue with non-enemy countries, although methods had to change. It was not possible to send travellers with large

12

cases of samples. In 1917, £23,500 worth of debts from enemy countries were written off and the following year nearly £20,000 worth of Russian debts were similarly treated.

A poignant example of the company's involvement with the war, apart from the men killed in the fighting, is mentioned in the board's minutes of November 1, 1918. C. F. Daft and his son, who had been employed as travellers in Ireland, were killed when the Irish mail steamship *Leinster* was torpedoed by a German submarine.

Peace brought a brief boom for the lace trade and in 1919 Thomas Adams Ltd was able to pay £1 bonus on each ordinary share — and in February the firm rejected a takeover bid. J. L. Litchfield tried to negotiate for the purchase of the business on behalf of a financial group prepared to put "a very large sum of money into the lace trade." The board rejected the offer, declaring the company's position was so strong and profits so high that there was little inducement to join a combination.

By January, 1921, however, the board were wondering whether to cut wages because of a slump in trade. By May, the weekly paid men were working one week on, one week off.

In 1921-2 a loss of £48,526 was incurred and in 1924, the Midland Bank, concerned about the company's overdraft, pressed the firm to improve its financial position. In 1925 the Sherwood Hill works were sold for £65,000 and a windfall arrived when £31,465 enemy debts previously written off were recovered.

Other economy measures included letting 30-40,000 sq feet of the Stoney Street premises to Boots for storage, selling a forge and cottage at St Mary's Gate for £1,700 and closing the New York office. Finally in 1927 the board had to abandon a long cherished principle that not more than two directors could be appointed from outside the company. Sir Ernest Jardine, President of Nottingham Chamber of Commerce, was asked to become a director and chairman of the board.

Sir Ernest, a leading local industrialist, was the son of John Jardine, a Yorkshireman who came to Nottingham in the 1850s to set up a successful business making lace machinery.

Sir Ernest's dynamism was soon felt and he launched what was intended to be a recovery plan. But subsequent minutes of the board reveal differences of opinion between the chairman and the other directors, culminating in September, 1930 in four of them offering to resign. Instead Sir Ernest did not seek re-election to the board.

Trade was still precarious and matters were not helped in December, 1930 when the board learned that a firm in Brazil, who owed Thomas Adams £23,713, had had their warehouse and other premises burned by revolutionaries.

Influenced by the general depression, the board decided to curtail export business and reduce its capital. The re-arranged company managed to achieve a small surplus of £1,185 for 1932 and continued to make modest profits until 1938 when there was a loss of £47. The daily services had been gradually discontinued but the firm still held services each January to honour their founder.

13

Soon after the outbreak of World War Two, Thomas Adams was requisitioned by the Ministry of Aircraft Production and given Government contracts to make items such as mosquito netting. This proved profitable. The firm also became a member of British Lace Furnishings under a scheme for the concentration of lace curtain manufacture.

But Thomas Adams found it difficult to re-establish on a peace time basis and the installation of new machinery and other improvements was delayed until 1950.

The trade itself was changing rapidly with the introduction of new synthetic yarns, new products and faster machines. New markets were opening up in Japan and the Far East.

Most of the early post-war production of lace had been directed by Government for export to earn foreign currency. From 1950 onwards the industry was free to make its own way.

But Thomas Adams had failed to adapt. The firm was bought out in 1954 and lace finishing ceased at the Stoney Street building . . . a sad end to the empire established by a remarkable man.

CHAPTER THREE

Early Days by Jack Richards

In 1913 all looked set fair for the Richards. My father had built a lovely house in Albemarle Road, Woodthorpe and named it Portreath after the Cornish town from where his family originated. After learning lace management at one of Nottingham's most famous firms, Thomas Adams, he had built up his own thriving business, E. and A. Richards.

Father was 45 when he married, somewhat older than mother. Their wedding in 1910 was a big one for those times. The ceremony was conducted by my grandfather, William H. Maude, who was a Methodist minister at his home church in West Kirby, near Liverpool. Later family photographs show grandfather as a missionary in West Africa — a fine figure of a man with a flowing white beard.

I was five when my father died in October, 1918. A few months previously the Liberal Party approached my mother about him becoming the next Sheriff of Nottingham. But she knew his illness was too serious and declined on his behalf. Father died from cancer of the throat — there was no treatment in those days. It was a very sad and early end for a man who had already achieved much and would undoubtedly have achieved much more had he lived. After father's death, many of the responsibilities fell on mother's shoulders. For the next 11 years, the firm was in the hands of managers — and the less said about that period the better.

After much thought it was decided that at 16 I should leave Nottingham High School to join the family business. Our premises in the Old Town Hall buildings, I recall, were like a rabbit warren. The structure shook when trains rumbled by to Victoria Station and the steps beside the building went down to Garners Hill and Broad Marsh. It was a place where policemen patrolled in pairs at night but it was also a useful short cut to Meadow Lane, home of Notts County, the oldest club in the Football League. All our girls worked on the second floor where the lace was finished, jennied and carded. The office and packing rooms were on the first floor and this is where I started business life in 1929.

They were very difficult years. After the slump of the 20s, the industry

15

was fighting for existence. Fortunately we had a very faithful employee in Leslie Bayliss, who taught me the trade. I took over the business in 1934 when I was 21. There was widespread unemployment and creditors were lining up at the door. Many doubted whether I could made a success of it at my age. But they were patient and we quickly paid off debtors by selling some stock.

But the bank was still breathing down my neck, restricting me to a £200 overdraft. My friend Albert Carter suggested moving our account to another bank, which gave me an overdraft of £500.Within a year we were in the black and never looked back.

My next task was to get a new range together. We had no machines of our own. Our side of the business was finishing lace, mostly for firms making up lingerie. At that time much of our trade was in embroidery — a yoke and two motifs embroidered on satin made what was known as a set.

I started travelling to London and built up some good contacts.The firms usually took a long time haggling over the price. But I knew when they reached a certain point they were going to buy.I held out above a rock bottom price, below which I couldn't go. A copper or two above I counted as a success. To this day I am never happier than on a sales mission. But between the wars no firm of our size did any overseas travelling. The system of exporting to South America, Mexico and so on was by commissioning houses like Thomas Adams, Simon May and Stiebel. Your range was sent overseas by the houses, who received 25 per cent to cover their expenses. All you had was a number. I still recall our Simon May order number — 87/-.

I was married in 1938. Leslie Bayliss looked after the business while Marjorie and I went on honeymoon to the Isle of Wight. When I returned I tried to have our rent at Weekday Cross reduced because the building was so dirty. The agent wouldn't hear of it. So we moved to Short Hill. But these premises proved expensive. So we moved again . . . and, for once, luck was in our favour. During the war Short Hill was blitzed. We went back to try and find our old safe, which had been too heavy to shift. But it was buried too deep in the rubble. With it had gone a chunk of the history of E. and A. Richards.

During the early years of the war, I was on reserve, keeping the business ticking over until 1942 when I was posted to the Maryhill Barracks, Glasgow, where I spent the coldest night of my life. Soon afterwards I was laid low by vaccine fever. I joined the Royal Corps of Signals and was posted to Scarborough. When the Second Front started I was dodging doodlebugs in Tilbury before being sent East in 1944.

When the war was over I returned to find the business just about solvent, hardly any money in the kitty and hardly any stock. On the little quota business we were allowed we had to manage. I was pleading for the restrictions to be lifted.

It was the most frustrating period of my life. No matter how hard you wanted to work there was no work to do. I recall some very lively dominoe sessions during long coffee breaks in the Khardoma Cafe in

16

8: Weekday Cross. Close to this sign was the front entrance of E. and A. Richards original building.

Clumber Street with journalist Arthur Turner and a few other friends.

About this time we moved from Stoney Street to even smaller premises in High Pavement. E. and A. Richards had sunk to its lowest ebb. But there was a silver lining when Walter Bruckmann sought me out. A German Jew, who had fled the Nazi purge and settled in South Africa, he came to Europe seeking agencies. I was in London but he had heard of my progress and left his phone number in Holland. I seized the opportunity and that phone call changed my life and led to extensive overseas travel.

I knew we had to export to survive. The market had changed. Firms were no longer prepared to be at the mercy of the commission houses. Direct selling was now the name of the enterprise and I was one of the first to travel to South Africa to sell lace in 1949.

With increased business our premises were too small. We moved to 16 Bottle Lane in Nottingham's narrowest thoroughfare. We were on the first floor and Johnson's Travel Agency, who were to prove such a good ally, were on the ground floor. To book my overseas trips I simply walked downstairs. Around this time Rex Mellers joined me to run the office. We quickly outgrew Bottle Lane and in 1950 moved to St Mary's Place. There we were joined by Frank Starkey and my son Michael. It was the happiest and most successful period of my business life.

We had come a long way from the trains rumbling by Weekday Cross. I often visit the area today en route to business appointments as chairman of Nottingham Lace Centre. Our old premises are no more. The area has been cleverly re-created by the City Council as a little garden retreat. On warm days it's a pleasant place to sit . . . and a whole host of memories come flooding back, of experiences and adventures around the world and most all the characters of our famous old Nottingham lace trade.

18

CHAPTER FOUR

More Adventures of a Lace Exporter

(i) NEW ZEALAND

The firm flourished after our move to St Mary's Place in 1950. The previous year I made my first export trip by air to South Africa and this whetted my appetite for further overseas travel. So January, 1952 found me again at London Airport ready for an evening take-off. Again the airline was BOAC and I was bound for New Zealand and Australia, via New York, Toronto, San Francisco, Vancouver, Honolulu and Fiji. There was no Concorde then, consuming vast distances at twice the speed of sound. The flight to New York alone took over 20 hours, including a freezing stop for re-fuelling in Iceland in mid-winter and an unscheduled landing at Caledon in Nova Scotia to head off a tornado in our flight-path. Vancouver to Honolulu was a long, long night flight over the Pacific by Skymaster. So imagine our joy at landing in Honolulu and being booked for a 24-hour stopover at the Moana Hotel, next to Waikiki Beach.

After this fantastic break, all at the expense of Canadian Pacific Airways, we took off in the darkness and headed for Canton Island and Fiji, where the airline gave us another day's rest.

We landed soon after breakfast and were taken around the island in buses for some sightseeing and bathing. Fijian schoolchildren sang to us, including God Save the Queen — a charming and touching tribute to Britain, which made us feel quite homesick. We also enjoyed the luscious fruits of this lovely island, which is now rapidly developing as a tourist resort.

Twenty five years later I was talking to a fellow passenger as we waited for our flight to Suva. He had bought a huge tract of land along the coast and left it lying there for two decades or more. Now, in 1977, he was a Canadian millionaire and had been in Fiji to supervise the building of one more luxury hotel on the island. Such is the difference between a far-sighted business magnate and the travelling lace man!

I was now on the last leg of my journey — a night flight to Auckland. The old airport there became a firm favourite of mine. I was met by my good friend Stan Amos and his wife, who planned to drive me through

19

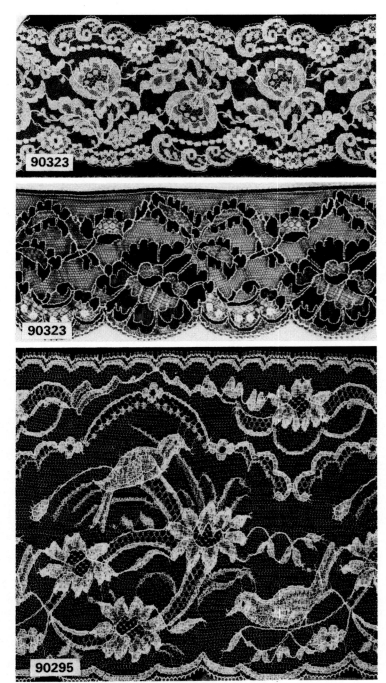

9: Three exquisite Leavers laces.

10: Comparable laces in Raschel (top pattern) and Leavers.

the spectacular scenery of Rotorua on our way to Wellington, where Stan's lingerie business was based.

Soon after my arrival, I was laid low by a highly unpleasant fever — the only illness I contracted in all my trips. But I was wonderfully nursed by an elderly maid at the old Queen's Hotel, Auckland. Within 48 hours I was able to resume work and landed one of the biggest orders of my life. I immediately felt much better and continued in Auckland doing good business. The agent working with me, Alf Bolland, ran Stan's Auckland office and suggested I might like to go hunting wild boar with him. I didn't feel quite up to such active and hazardous sport. So we finished off the business in Auckland about midweek and set off by car towards Wellington. We were to spend the weekend at Rotorua and booked into a hotel near one of the sulphur springs. But I was still feeling so weak that it took me all my time to survive the sulphuric smell, which permeated the rooms.

So the boiling mud and wonderful sights of Rotorua held less fascination for me. But I enjoyed a boat trip on the lake, where I could breathe fresh, sweet air and being introduced to the famous Maori guide Rangi. I also vividly recall a marvellous musical evening, culminating in the Maori song, *Now is the Hour*, later made famous by Gracie Fields. There is nothing more haunting than to hear it in its natural, original setting.

In Wellington I stayed in Stan's lovely house and he arranged many appointments for me so that the trip became a great financial success. We discussed the formation of a lace wholesale business in Wellington and I was introduced to our future accountant, Cuth Hogg, chairman of the famous All Blacks.

Having exhausted the possibilities in Wellington, I travelled by Dakota to the South Island, where I was to link up with Stan's manager in Dunedin — Howard Smith, a jovial character and still a very good friend. After a couple of days' business in Dunedin, Howard and I set off by road for Christchurch. Dunedin is a town more Scottish than Aberdeen if that is possible. Founded by the Scots, it has many statues of Robert Burns and as we left snow was beginning to fall. The country was wild and beautiful. But suddenly the car stopped abruptly. Howard had observed that I had dropped asleep, a common habit of mine in a car when I am not driving. He told me I had not come all that way to miss the superb scenery and suggested I drive. So I took the wheel and we had not gone far when I rounded a corner to find the road covered by thousands of sheep. It took an hour or so to thread our way through them. A lorry behind the huge flock contained the corpses of three or four dead sheep, struck, no doubt, by lorries rounding bends too fast.

After a couple of calls in the town of Timaru, we were off again through the rolling Canterbury countryside with sheep and still more sheep in every direction. But Howard was not looking for sheep. I was driving again and he suddenly said: "Stop Jack for a few minutes." From the boot of the car he took a rifle and advanced into a field, where he shot a rabbit — for dinner, he said. So here was a travelling salesman who also knew his way around the countryside. Another insight into New Zealand life.

Christchurch is as English in character as Dunedin is Scottish. The beauty and tranquillity of these lovely islands has to be seen to be believed. New Zealand often gives me a feeling of wide, open spaces, particularly the South Island, and when I came to walk the path from Port Lyttleton over the hills to Christchurch, a plaque told me that it was only 100 years since the first settlers took that route.

Today it is still a wonderful place to visit. A few years later Marjorie accompanied me on a visit and we borrowed the firm's car for a 10-day tour of the South Island. We stayed two days at the Hermitage Hotel, Mount Cook and had an exciting flight by Cessna Aircraft around the mountain. The Southern Alps compare very favourably with their more famous European counterparts. The plane, fitted with skis, landed on a glacier, which was strange to walk on. We then flew round the mountain and just as it became very bumpy, the pilot spotted an avalanche and turned the plane towards the mountain for us to observe this remarkable sight. We were glad, however, when he headed back to base as the turbulence was tremendous. Later we heard that two climbers from the hotel had been lost that day in an avalanche. Was it the one we saw?

We continued to Queenstown, where it is possible to make an even more exiting flight to Milford but the weather closed in and I have never made this trip.

Our friendship with the Amos's led to many happy occasions. They brought Stan's sister and brother-in-law — Lily and Arthur Hopkins — on one trip to Britain. Marjorie and I went to London to meet them. They were great fun and were staying at the Grosvenor Hotel. They told us to bring a toothbrush and stay the night, which we did. They booked us in and after spending the night in the West End we returned to the hotel to find we had been allocated one of the luxury suites. I always remember the Hopkins dashing down the corridor with toilet rolls to welcome "the bridal couple." This was a wonderful night and the next morning we had breakfast in the suite and were accorded the full treatment by the Grosvenor House staff.

Stan came to Nottingham and gave a talk to the Woodthorpe Forum, my debating society. This was an evening members present always remember. Stan remained active in his business until his recent death in his 80s.

During my first trip to New Zealand I had made several lifelong friends. And as Stan and I talked and planned on that last evening at his home in Wellington, I looked back on a trip already a tremendous financial success. I went to bed very happy, eagerly looking forward to an early flight by seaplane from Wellington Harbour to Sydney, Australia.

(ii) AUSTRALIA

On the day I was to make my first trip to Australia, I breezed into breakfast to be greeted with some stunning news: severe import restrictions had been imposed. But that blow could not detract from the thrill of taking off in a flying boat from Wellington Harbour and flying over the Tasman Sea to Australia. We touched down in Rose Bay and I had my first glimpse of Australia. I am amazed that the airlines have not persevered with flying boats. My flight in 1949 from Victoria Falls to Southampton and then from Wellington to Sydney still ranks as the most interesting I have made.

It was three years before I made another trip and with many relatives in Sydney and Melbourne, I always had people to see. Most of my business was in Melbourne and the districts surrounding this great city but it was always worthwhile to visit Sydney, Brisbane, Adelaide and Perth.

Whilst in Melbourne my agents took me to country towns with big factories such as Ballarat and Bendigo. These trips were full of interest, especially Bendigo, named after the famous Nottingham boxer and the centre of Australia's gold rush many years ago. One can still see the old mine workings on the edge of the town.

Dandenong is another town just outside Melbourne, where two Nottingham lace firms, W. H. Smith and G. W. Price, established factories to make Barmen laces. The Smith family came from Castle Donington, grandfather Smith being famous for inventing the porcupine roller for lace machines. His son Arthur emigrated to Australia with the firm and settled in Dandenong, where he bought land which is now worth a small fortune. His sons Terry and Alan are still running the business in Melbourne and I have spent many happy times with them.

One of the main aims of my visits was to find the right agents in the territory and it took quite a few trips before I finally got together with Bob Baenziger in Melbourne. Bob is a livewire in the lace game in Australia and still represents E. A. Richards in that part of the world.

Overseas travel gives one the opportunity of holidays in exotic places. Marjorie and I have visited Bangkok, Hongkong and Singapore on our way to Australia, apart from some of the places I will describe later. In Australia our daughter Gwenneth joined us for her 21st birthday. After my business in Brisbane was finished we all flew to Hayman Island, just off the Queensland coast, to have a look at the Barrier Reef.

Normally the tide leaves the reef clear of water at certain times but that day there was still a foot or two left on the reef. Two boats went out from Hayman Island and they put us on the reef but we were too busy trying to keep our feet to see much. Finally we became separated. Marjorie and I were hauled back on to our boat but Gwenneth was left stranded for the second boat to rescue her. It was a strange feeling to sail away and see her standing in the middle of the sea with a few other people but they all turned up at the hotel later in the evening. Our boat kept breaking down, it was very wet and cold and we were very late getting back to the hotel. So late we had missed our dinner. Not one of our most successful jaunts but we had seen plenty of beautiful coral and we can say we have walked on the Barrier Reef . . . just.

A more successful trip was made by Marjorie and I a few years earlier when we took a Roylan Cruise around the Barrier Reef Islands. The boats were quite small but one lived on board. Marjorie will tell you it was certainly the roughest holiday she has had. Nevertheless we saw many interesting places and in one spot went ashore and plucked oysters from the rocks. They were dipped in the sea and swallowed by our tough Australian friends. Unfortunately I cannot report finding any pearls.

Usually I completed my business and took some holiday on the way home. These business trips to Australia and New Zealand were very tough going particularly Melbourne where I stayed three weeks on occasions and when Marjorie started coming with me she found this part of the journey very hard going as I was working from 8am until 6pm and then most evenings were spent entertaining customers. So it was very hard going for about two months and a short holiday at the end was not only a just reward but a very necessary one.

11: Sydney Opera House and Bridge by night.

During my first visits to Australia, friends would take me down to the Harbour in Sydney and show me the plans for a wonderful opera house they hoped to build. Sydney Harbour is extensive and very beautiful with numerous homes nestling in its little bays. I have many relatives in that area with whom I have stayed from time to time. After working through a very hot and humid day in the city, it was a great pleasure to go down to the quay and take a ferry home in the evening. The fresh sea air on the harbour blew away all the humidity. At one time our good friends, Percy and Doris Wilkins, had a lovely house overlooking the Harbour in which both Marjorie and I have stayed.

The Sydney Harbour Bridge is a landmark and a remarkable achievement in itself, carrying the railway and several lanes of traffic to many of the suburbs. Just near the sea terminal and the ferry berths and close to the bridge, it was proposed to build the world's finest opera house and concert hall.

In the early 50s we looked at the plans and then work started. I was visiting Australia every other year through the building period. They had all sorts of trouble with the design of the building and a change of architect which delayed things for many years. It began to look as though it would never be finished. Money was never the main obstacle as

Australia has had its Golden Caskets and other prize draws far longer than we have had Ernie. Much of the revenue from these funds went towards the Opera House.

Gradually the project took shape and its three great wings were finally completed making the building look like a great bird at the side of the harbour. At last it was opened and on my penultimate trip I went to a concert. On my last trip in 1979 it was a great treat to hear Joan Sutherland singing in her native Sydney in The Merry Widow.

Today no visitor to Australia should fail to visit this latest wonder of the world. It has its own first class restaurant and self service cafe and one is always within sight of the harbour and the harbour bridge. I have happy memories of sailing in the harbour with friends like Percy Wilkins and a relative Dr Rowley Richards.

(iii) FIJI AND HONOLULU

Most of my trips to Australia and New Zealand began in Perth and ended in Auckland but several times I started in Africa, visiting Nairobi, Victoria Falls, Bulawayo and Salisbury. I then moved on to Johannesburg, Cape Town, Port Elizabeth, East London and Durban before taking a plane to Mauritius and on to the Cocos Islands and Perth. That added up to a six-week trip before starting the main business. Having done several of these long trips on my own I was able to make them so successful that I could afford to take Marjorie with me, which made all the travel so much more relaxing from my point of view.

One return journey particularly stands out in my memory. Seen off from Auckland by Bob and Nancy Barnett after dealing with Richards Laces in New Zealand, we took a plane landing at Fiji, where some business was gained selling lace to Indian stores on the island. We came down to breakfast in a hotel stunned by the news that President Kennedy had been assassinated. We went out looking at coral and sugar plantations but everywhere the atmosphere was very sombre. It was as though the Fijians and Indians had lost a personal friend.

In Suva I liked to stay at a hotel called the Trade Winds, beside the Pacific, where one met many interesting characters, particularly ocean yachtsmen. Having dinner there one night, I was spellbound by a tropical thunderstorm out at sea. This awesome display of natural lighting effects was better than any firework display. On another occasion I leaned over the rail outside the hotel to marvel at the shoals of beautiful, coloured fish attracted by the hotel lights. Fiji, with its Indian bazaars, its coral, sugar cane, bananas and charming children is truly enchanting. But beware of the mosquitoes!

Honolulu is another beautiful island. Sadly it is now something of a concrete jungle — very different from the way I found it on my first visit in 1951. By day we relaxed on the surfboards and the catamarans on Waikiki and with dinner at night in the company of Cuth and Eileen Hogg life really seemed worth living. We also booked a flight to see most of the other Hawaiian islands. The 5am start from the hotel proved well worthwhile because the trip produced an enthralling experience — flying

26

12: Waikiki Beach, Hawaii.

over an erupting volcano on the main island of Hawaii.

I was glad to be in the larger of the two planes which made the trip. We flew at a decent height and watched the smaller plane fly right down into the crater, where molten lava was pouring over the lip of the volcano and down its sides.

Breakfasting at a beautiful hotel beside the Pacific with exotic tropical flowers all around, we thanked the lace industry for giving us the chance to make these wonderful trips around the world.

We arrived back at our hotel in Honolulu late in the evening and the next day everything came to a standstill during the television coverage of President Kennedy's funeral. The whole country mourned. Only one trip was possible and it seemed appropriate on such a day to travel by catamaran to Pearl Harbour. Many battleships still lie below the water

13. Royal Hawaiian Hotel

and it is difficult to imagine the hell that broke loose when Japan attacked in 1942.

There is much so much to do in Honolulu. I have seen the QE2 in harbour. Watching her sail, one felt proud to be an Englishman. There are tours into the hills and the display of dolphins are bigger and better than anywhere in the world. Sitting by the sea, listening to lilting Hawaiian music, we savoured every possible moment.

As one travels around the world it is often quite easy to spot people known as residents. Having lost their partners in life they prefer, and can obviously afford, to stay in hotels where they have comfort and company. A favourite haunt of mine for a pre-lunch drink in Honolulu has long been the vast circular bar on the beach at the Royal Hawaiian. On one occasion a few years ago I was seated next to a quite imposing gentleman who did not offer any conversation. I had just arrived from New Zealand and feeling rather tired. So we sipped our drinks silently but obviously aware of each other's presence.

The next day I arrived to find there was only one empty seat next to this same gentleman. I sat down, ordered my gin and tonic from the Chinese barman, who has been there as long as I remember. Taking my courage in my hands I addressed my companion and having broken the ice found him quite forthcoming.

He explained he was a retired accountant from New York, who had lived at the hotel for several years. He indicated his bedroom window overlooking the sea and said it had always been his ambition to be a resident of the Royal Hawaiian. Sipping his gin and tonic, he told me he could recommend the life. "Of course," he calmly added, "you do need to have a fairly large income to be able to do this!"

I reflected with some wonderment what his fairly large income must amount to. Then to my surprise, he added: "There are seven residents at this hotel and we are all to be found by the pool in the mornings." I was invited to join the "residents de luxe" at one of the world's greatest hotels.

My last visit was in 1979 and I missed my old friend at the bar. So I enquired after him from the Chinese barman, who said: "Oh yes, he is still here but his doctor has forbidden gin and tonics. So he does not come to the bar anymore." He told me I would find him by the pool but somewhat older and I gathered becoming senile. I did not pursue the contact but I am still convinced that becoming a resident of the Royal Hawaiian must be the ultimate in retirement.

CHAPTER FIVE
Cowcatchers and All

(i) SAN FRANCISCO

San Francisco is always a delight to visit. Our Pam Am flight from Honolulu arrived in early evening with the great land mass of America gradually appearing after countless miles of water. Below myriads of lights came into view as the plane began the spectacular descent to the airport.

Whenever possible I break my journey here for a couple of nights on the way from New Zealand. Chinatown seems another world as you stroll between the stores full of ivory, jade and Chinese novelties. Not far away the cable cars climb the incredibly steep hills, passengers hanging on to all sides. The end of the line is Fisherman's Wharf, where fresh fish can be enjoyed in one of the excellent restaurants hugging the harbour. A visit here is a "must" for the tourist.

You need a head for heights on the Golden Gate Bridge, spanning the entrance to San Francisco Harbour. It's so high that it is often in cloud. But on the other side of the bridge is a different world, where woodlands of towering Red Californian pine provide a peaceful retreat after the noise and bustle of the busy city.

Back again over the bridge, you have an unforgettable view of the skyline of the great city and, if you are lucky, an ocean liner sailing below looks like a toy ship. Offshore lies the forbidding and the infamous prison of Alcatraz, much too far from the mainland for a swim to be easily accomplished.

But alas it was time to go and little did Marjorie and I realise what lay ahead. We were in the middle of a scenic journey home from New Zealand via Fiji, Honolulu, San Francisco. All had gone well to that point. Our next target was Vancouver where we were due to spend the night before boarding the Canadian Pacific train through the Rockies to Calgary.

On a beautiful afternoon we boarded a United Airlines plane for Seattle, where we had to change planes for Vancouver. As we approached Seattle the weather deteriorated and, for nearly an hour, we circled the airport, flying blind in cloud. Then the pilot announced he was going to try and land, so down we went and felt rather than saw the landing. The fog was dense and we had missed our connection, which had managed to take off before we landed.

We were given the choice of continuing to Vancouver by bus in the fog or spending the night in a hotel near the airport and hopefully flying to Vancouver the next morning. It was already dark and a bus journey under those conditions had no appeal. We elected to stay in Seattle for the night — at least we had a comfortable room and a good meal. Our main worry was our booking on the train the following evening out of Vancouver.

The next day dawned just as bad as the previous one or even worse. The airport was closed and remained closed. I was told our only hope was to go by train and there was one due in Vancouver in time for us to make the connection. All hope of Marjorie seeing the beautiful city of Vancouver had already vanished as we were told the belt of fog extended right up the coast.

So our next journey was by bus to the railway station and we finally left Seattle without seeing anything whatsoever of it. Never have I known a railway journey so slow. We crept along through the fog, mile after mile until we were running over two hours late. I began to realise we would not make the connection in Vancouver and so I talked to the conductor, a jovial negro, who confirmed there was no hope. But he had an idea. The last stop before Vancouver was within five miles of the station where the Canadian Pacific train would make its first stop. If we were lucky enough to find a taxi we could still do it. Another lady listening to my conversation said that she and two friends were also booked on the same train. Could they join us? Naturally we said yes.

So just before 7.30pm we were deposited in the darkness with all our luggage. There was no real platform. Amazingly a taxi emerged from the gloom and we told the driver where we wanted to go. He said we must all pile into his cab with all our luggage as he was the only taxi on the road that night. He agreed the other station was five miles away — if he could find it. We had to take cases on our knees but somehow or other we all got in and began another nerveracking journey. A curse from the driver's seat told us something had happened. The fog was so dense he had overshot the station so we had to turn round and go back. Fortunately we seemed to have the road to ourselves.

Much to our relief we finally drew up in front of a wooden building. We were taken along the track to a shack . . . a waiting room which turned out to be something straight out of a Wild West film. Huddled around a huge stove in the middle of the room were our fellow passengers swathed in furs. The night was bitter as well as foggy. Within minutes a loud blast announced the arrival of our train — complete with cow catcher on the front — chugging through the fog. It was quite the most amazing connection any of us had made.

The conductor appeared from the train, checked our tickets and took us to our reserved sleeper just as though we had joined the train in Vancouver. Nobody seemed at all surprised and soon we were ordering our evening meal. The train, steam driven in those days, chuffed off into the night and into the Rocky Mountains.

After a good night's sleep we woke to find ourselves in a winter wonderland with magnificent views of the snow-clad mountains. We finally stopped at Banff, a famous resort in the Rockies. The rest of the day made the journey all worthwhile and by late afternoon we arrived at Calgary. Here we had a few hours rest before joining our plane to fly to Edmonton and then through the night to Toronto, where the lace business beckoned us again.

(ii) AFRICA

Sometimes you need the qualities of an explorer to survive experiences abroad. Staying in the Queen's Hotel in Cape Town on one of my early trips to South Africa, I went to my room one night — and was confronted by four huge eyes staring at me. This was the first time I had seen cockroaches this big. They just sat in the middle of the floor and defied me.

They were so big I did not have the courage to squash them. So we just stood and looked at one another. Finally I went to the porter for help but they were too used to cockroaches to worry and when I returned to my room, they had gone. I could not find a hole large enough for them but I did not look too carefully and I never saw them again.

I have happier memories of Cape barbeques. With Table Mountain as a backcloth, these brais, as they are known locally, are something to savour and special areas are set aside for them. There is also a wonderful scenic drive along the coast leading to Cape Point, the Cape of Good Hope.

A great thrill on a calm day is to take a cable car to the top of Table Mountain, which is so steep at the end it seems impossible you will make it. But you do — and are rewarded by one of the world's great views. Below lies Cape Town climbing up the moutainside and ships in the harbour look like toys.

Moving a little to the left you can look towards Cape Point and a few more steps brings the Indian Ocean into view. A short walk and you can look back across the Cape Flats, with Cape Town's Airport in the middle, over 30 miles to the Drakenstein Mountains, where most of the beautiful vineyards are situated. A notable exception is Constantia, Simon Van de Stel's original home, which lies in the most beautiful setting to the rear of Table Mountain right under Devil's Peak.

To the Atlantic side of Table Mountain is another well known landmark of the Cape, Lion's Head, a hill with its summit very much like a lion. Right at it's base by the side of the ocean was the Queen's Hotel, which is now converted into a modern five-star hotel. We also stayed many times at another of the Cape's prestigious hotels, the Mount Nelson, which formerly belonged to the Union Castle, a marvellous shipping line that sadly is no longer in operation. We class the Mount

*18: **Barmen lace machine.***

and, in fact, became quite a force in the company. Alas, for some unknown reason, his health did not stand up to the strain and like my father, for different reasons, the good times did not last long.

And so life became political as so often happens in big groups. Never my strongest point. I have always been best at the purely commercial side

19: Mr Ronald G. Walton, Director of the British Lace Federation and Miss Gwendolen Crisp, who was a long serving Deputy Secretary of the Federation, examine the lace and embroidery to be presented to the Queen.

20: The Lord Mayor presents the lace to the Queen at the Council House, May 1968.

21: The first woman Lord Mayor of Nottingham, Coun Mrs Joan Case looking at a famous lace panel with Mr Bill Spowage.

22: Lace curtain machine with twisthand.

of the business. The famous firm of Levin Brothers had joined Selincourt before us and we were followed by Martin and Holliwell, bringing into the firm as colleagues Philip Holliwell and that remarkably effervescent character Peggy Wilkins. Through my legal connections with Bill Tyzack, I introduced Sir Geoffrey Barnett to Lou Levin and two or three years after E. and A. Richards had taken two floors in Delbeta House, the firm of Dobson and M. Browne became part of Selincourt.

Certainly the future looked most promising but it was not to last for the Richards' family. Another well known man in the trade, Cedric Wood had also joined us. He had been part of Jersey Kapwood, a firm which his famous father Alex Wood helped to found. Cedric brought a first class plant of Leavers machines into Selincourt as part of E. and A. Richards and, to this day, has proved most beneficial. But Cedric himself did not stay long any more than did my old friend Stan Wallis with whom I had formed Wallis and Richards.

Much could be written of this period. Better, I feel, to draw a veil over the next few years and merely record that in 1970, by mutual consent, I severed my connection with our old firm and with Selincourt. For the next nine years, I found a new home with Simon May and Co. At that time they had run into difficulties with their Lace Division and old friends such as Avril Allen and Geoffrey Hampson offered an opportunity much to my liking. Here I met another old lace trade friend in Jack Baker and also became very friendly with his younger brother, Malcolm. With a very sound inside man in Bill Robinson, we soon began to get the lace side of Simon May really ticking again. And so it remained until I retired in 1979 at the age of 66.

(i) LACE IN EUROPE

Many years ago the machine lace making countries of Europe formed their own organisation to discuss ideas and trends affecting the trade. Delegates from France, Germany, Great Britain, Spain, Austria, Switzerland and Italy meet bi-annually for a three-day conference hosted by one of the member countries. Celebride has three main sections, Lace (Dentelles), Curtains (Rideaux) and Embroidery (Broderie). Each of these sections meets about twice a year to discuss their own particular problems and prepare for the main bi-annual conference.

During the last 20 years of my business career I had close connections with Celebride. Britain was an associate member for many years but finally we became full members. During that period I was one of the delegates from the British Lace Federation and for my last four years until retirement I was chairman of the Lace (Dentelles) section. For two of these years from 1977 to 1979 Britain had the happy experience of also providing the Celebride President — John Walker, who afterwards received the MBE for his services to the industry. In those years substantial progress was made but it was an expensive business belonging to Celebride and gradually pressure was brought to bear from some quarters to bring about Britain's resignation as a full member. So all the good

49

work put in by John Walker, Ron Walton as our ever energetic secretary, myself and many others was lost. This was a great pity because I believe we always need to be able to talk to our competitors on the Continent. But the price was considered too high for the results achieved. Many happy memories remain, however, which will never be lost. Fairly frequent visits to interesting centres such as Paris, Zurich and Milan, brought a host of friends on the Continent.

I particularly recall one committee meeting in Milan. After completing some business for my firm in Stuttgart, I caught a morning flight and landed in Milan in quite thick fog. Geoffrey Fletcher, the other British delegate, was due to fly from London and join me there. By the time I had booked into my hotel, had lunch and made my way to the meeting, it became obvious that Geoff's flight had been delayed by fog. So the meeting started without him.

About 4pm it was announced that a strike had hit Milan. The airport was already closed and just at that moment Geoff appeared through the door. Evidently he had landed during a gap in the fog, before the strike took effect. The meeting was suspended while the energetic secretary Franco Bianchi made plans to change our return tickets to rail. We were then rushed round to the hotel to collect my bags and book me out (Geoff had never booked in). No problems were raised; they are used to strikes in Milan. Geoff and I, plus two Swiss delegates were dropped at the station and as we walked through the entrance a bottle shattered against the wall at the side of us. We accepted the strikers' parting gesture and quickly boarded the train to Zurich, which was still running.

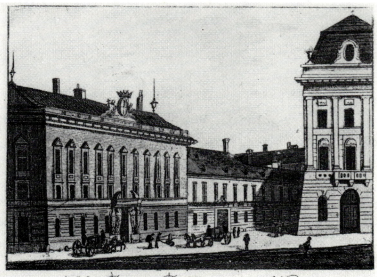

23: Venue for Celebride banquet in 1973.

Fortunately Milan is not far from the Swiss frontier but for those few miles the train seemed to crawl. There was no service and hardly a soul spoke. Then we were c r the border and the atmosphere changed beyond belief. The crew was Swiss and our Swiss friends escorted us to the restaurant car, where we spent the time passing through Lugano and the glorious scenery of the Alps, which was largely hidden from us in the night. A marvellous meal was served and we were a very contented party as the train drew into Zurich station towards midnight. Our friends found us a hotel and Geoff and I continued our journey home from Zurich the next day.

The bi-annual conferences of Celebride are splendid affairs. We have visited Venice, where we stayed on the Lido and Vienna, where the most wonderful meal was served in one of the ancient historical buildings. While the men had their conference, the ladies visited the Spanish Riding School and then most of us wound up the trip with a visit to the Opera House. Much beautiful lace is made in Vienna and through the good offices of Cedric Wood, I became quite friendly with Dr Hans Faber, who had a factory in the city. His brother Max managed their other factory in Turin. Happy are the memories of Vienna and the father of the Faber factory — Arthur Faber, who came to Nottingham to speak at the dinner of the Lace Federation while I was president.

The Swiss gave us a wonderful conference. Meetings were held in St Gallen and I particularly remember one excursion. Drinks were available as soon as we stepped aboard a train and it was a lovely summer's evening as we wound our way up the mountain to the beautiful village of Appenzell. There we were greeted by the arrival of the local herd of cows with their inevitable bells ringing and the shepherds and followers all in traditional Swiss costume. The procession made its way into the village, where we were escorted to a local hostelry for a sumptuous meal. Marjorie and I stayed a night in Appenzell some years later but gone was the atmosphere of that magical evening.

When Spain hosted the conference in Barcelona, we were entertained to dinner in the Maritime Hall, which was a special honour. We inspected the remarkable galleon housed there and the dinner was out of this world. When the business of the conference was concluded our Spanish host entertained us to lunch at his vineyards some 50 miles from Barcelona where we sampled his most excellent, sparkling wine — not permitted to be called Champagne, of course, but equally enjoyable.

Germany and France also hosted interesting conferences. The French secretary for many years and now treasurer is Franc Ginestou. Another leading French figure, who became a good friend with an excellent choice in cognac, is M. Bouvellain.

When the conference came to Britain, delegates were given a wonderful time. The Lord Mayor of Nottingham provided a Lace Ball at the Council House, when all the ladies were resplendent in their lace gowns and many of the men wore some form of lace as well. The second evening was a memorable one too in the majestic setting of Belvoir Castle. We staged a really first class fashion show and an excellent buffet. Our friends from the continent went home vowing that Britain was the "tops." The year I retired — 1979 — saw the second conference in England, held at Stratford-on-Avon with the main event at Warwick Castle. As always the lacemen of Europe enjoyed meeting one another and exchanging news of the industry. This proved to be my swan song in Celebride.

(ii) THE LACE CENTRE

As one chapter closed, little did I realise another was opening. Shortly after retiring in 1979 I was approached by Ruth Johns, then director of the Action Resource Centre, a charity which seconds business executives to community and employment projects. Ruth, who had obtained my name from the Retirement Bureau of the Institute of Directors, explained she was looking for a part-time small business consultant to work with the manager — yet to be appointed — in their new Nottingham office.

This proved to be yet another turning point in my life. In the summer of 1979 David Lowe arrived as manager — the start of a new and very valuable friendship. Together we found another good friend in ARC secretary Anne Pollard.

David and I worked closely together and I began to think seriously of trying to establish a dream I had fostered over many years — to provide the city with a centre where visitors could see and buy the best in Nottingham lace. So many people associate Nottingham with lace and throughout my years in the trade the question of where to buy lace arose time and again. John McMeeking of A. C. Gill and I had frequently suggested to the British Lace Federation that the city needed such a centre. Now the means existed by which the aim could be achieved. David and I noticed the City Council was running a competition called Heritage to bring forth ideas for the benefit of the city. We immediately entered and were awarded a prize for a projected Lace Centre.

The next necessity was to find a home for the centre. So we talked to the city's Arts Director Brian Loughbrough who had his office on the first floor of a beautiful medieval building dating back to the 15th century. This once housed a famous restaurant called Severns which had been situated in the Lace Market until it was moved timber by timber to its present position on Castle Road facing the Robin Hood statue. The removal was made in 1969-70 to make way for the Broad Marsh Centre.

Brian Loughbrough had searched for some years to find something suitable for the ground floor of this lovely old building. Both he and I agreed it would be ideal for a lace centre and the City Council agreed. So we went ahead. Now we needed to finance the venture. John McMeeking, always interested, gave his full support. I then approached several friends in the trade.

Henry Hurt of G. H. Hurt and Co immediately gave his support. Geoffrey Hampson, a very old friend and now chairman of Simon May and Co Ltd, felt sure his firm would support us and they did. John Walker, MBE, now chairman of Basford Dyers Co and an important lace curtain manufacturer, followed. I wanted to have my old firm represented

52

24: Civic party being welcomed by Jack Richards at the official opening of the Lace Centre in 1980.

25: The Lace Centre, which has been described as an Aladdin's Cave.

especially to obtain supplies of the lovely lace tablecloths, originally made by Martin and Holliwell and now marketed under the name of Filigree. To my delight Selincourt agreed and quite an interesting board was coming into being.

Alan Litman with his famous family business agreed to join us and so did Richard Granger, whose family has made the most beautiful Leavers and now Raschel laces over the years. John Mason, whose firm F. and C. Mason make the most famous Cluny Leavers laces and also many Raschels completed the team in what has proved to be a very happy and successful company. I was elected chairman and we have had excellent financial advice from accountant Keith Butler, who understands the lace industry by his connections with the British Lace Federation and the Lace Research Association.

So with this solid and impressive base we were ready to launch. I approached other firms in the trade but without any more success although I know that one or two of them now wish they had joined the organisation.

Our next move was to find a manager and here Action Resource Centre again proved invaluable. Mrs Dorothea Haythornthwaite had just retired from British Home Stores and, like me, was looking for something to do. So we got together and the management has been a great success in her hands. She introduced several ladies to the centre and our three part-time staff, Mrs Sheila Perrin, Mrs Margaret Magee (recently replaced by Mrs Joan Nagle) and Mrs Joan Butler are invaluable to us. Mrs Joan King is another great asset, responsible for display both inside and outside the centre.

So on August 1, 1980 we opened the doors and on August 13 we had a wonderful official civic opening by the Lord Mayor and his Lady accompanied by the Sheriff and his Lady and several councillors. We were well and truly launched and I feel the centre is now part of city life and, although small, we know that over 100,000 people a year visit us. Just round the corner in Castle Gate is the Costume Museum which has beautiful lace displays of great interest. So I feel that at last the city is able to present the lace industry at its best.

Meanwhile David Lowe has returned to his first career, journalism. But we teamed up again to write *The City of Lace*. Published by the Lace Centre, it immediately aroused great interest and I was very proud when Christina Foyle of the famous London bookshop, W. G. Foyle, offered me her art gallery for a lace display.

We had a wonderful month in London at Foyles — probably the best lace exhibition Joan King has created. It has also given my wife Marjorie and I a new interest. We have been invited to the famous Foyles literary luncheons at the Dorchester Hotel, which took us back to an old haunt of ours in the days of E. and A. Richards when we frequently stayed in that lovely hotel.

55

CHAPTER EIGHT
Lace Market Revival

Walk around the Lace Market and it's possible to see how Nottingham evolved from a Saxon settlement to an industrial quarter. The rectangular pattern of streets, covering just three acres, have survived from medieval times. As the centuries rolled by, this small area became a civic, commercial and spiritual focal point, containing the Town Hall, St Mary's Church, a theatre, early schools and charitable institutions. Also here were the Town Gaol and House of Correction and a vault beneath a house used by persecuted non-conformists before the passing of the Toleration Act.

In the 16th and 17th centuries many noble families built large mansions with gardens and orchards in what was to become a very fashionable part of the town. Little remains of this elegant period, except on High Pavement, where many 18th century buildings survive, including the classical Shire Hall. The first factories were built in the late 18th century, woven into this tight tapestry, with development centred mainly in the Hounds Gate and St Mary's Gate area. The burgesses refused to sanction building on common land. So large scale industrial expansion, after Heathcoat's invention of the first real lace machines in 1808, transformed Nottingham from a pleasant market town to an overcrowded place, crammed into a boundary bursting at the seams.

The name Lace Market first emerged in the early 19th century and the opening of the town's first railway in 1839 and the arrival of penny post in 1840 were of great benefit to the lace trade. The building of a new station in 1844 nearer to London Road possibly helped move the Lace Market away from Hounds Gate-Gastle Gate area to St Mary's Gate and Stoney Street. Certainly there was an explosion of factory building in the 1850s and 1860s. Two factors made this possible — the first was the release of the common land, following the Enclosure Act. The second was the increasing use of steam power for hosiery and lace manufacture. The grand houses were all destroyed and in their place rose vast warehouses, often deliberately grandiose to impress lace buyers.

The character of the area today derives almost entirely from this period. Tall warehouses, often four or five storeys high, give a canyon-like appearance to many of the streets, creating a tremendous sense of

56

scale and enclosure. The premises erected for one of the most influential figures of his day, Richard Birkin, were partly built on the site of Plumtre House, an 18th century mansion sold to Birkin in 1852 for £8,140. To accommodate the warehouse, a new street called Broadway was constructed, linking St Mary's Gate and Stoney Street. The building is still there with an archway entrance, over which are carved in stone a bee, a symbol of industriousness, together with the initials of the owner, architect and builder.

Broadway, although only just under 100 yards long, has a graceful curve in the centre. This was in keeping with the originality of the designs, both external and internal. The quality of the buildings reflect the fact that they were usually built as the headquarters of large lace concerns and it was here that the more skilled work and selling was done. Increasingly lace manufacture itself moved away from the Lace Market to outlying areas. As well as Watson Fothergill and T. C. Hine, other Nottingham architects involved in designing Lace Market warehouses were Samuel Dutton Walker, R. C. Sutton, W. A. Heazell, A. H. Goodall and A. N. Bromley.

At the peak of the trade, around 1914, the Lace Market boasted no fewer than 158 warehouses. But after the First World War, the lace industry went into a steep decline and many Leavers lace firms went out of business. It was a sign of the times when 56 High Pavement, a particularly fine 18th century house, became a public assistance office. Many of the grand warehouses were sub-divided and let off to small textile concerns. Rents were cheap and little was spent on maintenance. The Lace Market deteriorated into a decaying warren for dry goods, electrical suppliers, printers and the demolition men.

By the 1960s the Lace Market was very badly run down and plans for comprehensive redevelopment and the building of a network of new roads blighted the area. Properties in Barker Gate, Stoney Street and St Mary's Gate were demolished. It was intended to put a new road through Pilcher Gate to link up with redevelopment in the Broad Marsh area. Barker Gate was widened but the plan was not carried out further, leaving vacant eyesores between Stoney Street and St Mary's Gate. Further property was pulled down on Pilcher Gate and Fletcher Gate and the latter widened and joined up to a new relief road to Canal Street, with a new multi-storey car park on Pilcher Gate.

In the wake of the Civic Amenities Act, however, the Lace Market was designated in 1969 as one of the city's first conservation areas. A working party was established to draw up a new conservation policy for the area and this was published in 1973. Buildings essential to the character of the conservation area were identified and proposals made for the development and improvement of the very many derelict sites throughout the Lace Market.

The City Council adopted the new conservation strategy and the Land Committee voted a special fund for improvements. The City Planning Officer began a very difficult task of encouraging development and renovation in a run down area which many people saw merely as a grim legacy of the past.

Three of the larger derelict sites were developed for new housing, two by the City Council and one by a housing association. The fine new housing project in Halifax Place restored homes on a site which had been used for residential purposes for at least 1,000 years. What's more, it achieved a balance, matching the scale of adjoining commercial buildings and providing a desirable living environment in the heart of a busy, built-up area. The project, for the Bridge Housing Association, won a commendation in the 1980 Department of the Environment Good Housing Design Award for architects Cullen, Carter and Hill.

The council's enlightened policy of allowing archaeologists the opportunity to excavate sites before redevelopment was particularly rewarding at Halifax Place. It yielded a rich harvest of artefacts, including an iron staff head and a belt buckle from the 9th and 10th centuries.

Another successful restoration and refurbishment scheme at 15 Middle Pavement, on the fringe of the Lace Market, won a 1982 Civic Trust commendation for the Douglas Feast Partnership.

In the heart of the Lace Market itself, 31 formerly derelict sites or unmade car parks were landscaped. An outstanding achievement was the creation of the small but delightful Garnet's Hill Park from a vacant site, which once overlooked the slums of Narrow Marsh. This won Civic Trust and Times/RIC Conservation Award commendations.

Since 1976 over 100 buildings have been renovated with grant aid totalling £500,000 and the estimated total investment in the area, excluding new housing developments, is £3m. Work, financially assisted by the council and DoE, ranged from minor but essential repairs to roofs and windows to wholesale renovation and refurbishment. Examples include 16 Stoney Street, where a grant was approved for the external renovation of this prominent former warehouse, which has planning permission for conversion into offices, studios and workshops. At 1 Kayes Walk — a fascinating thoroughfare — grants were given for the external renovation of this Victorian warehouse and internal conversion to offices, design studios and exhibition use. In addition, many buildings have been cleaned, with impressive results.

An enterprising facelift also brought renewed vitality to the Hockley area. By the early 1970s formerly thriving shopping streets traversing the Lace Market like Carlton Street, Goosegate and Hockley itself had become very run down. By 1978 over half the shops were vacant. The City Planning Department organised a major scheme for the district as part of the inner area programme, which proved remarkably successful with nearly 30 buildings renovated. The Midland Group Gallery, one of the largest art complexes in the country, was established on Carlton Street with grant assistance from the City Council and other bodies. A number of new businesses are flourishing in the area too, including boutiques, restaurants, clubs, offices and studios. Conservation and enlightened redevelopment has transformed the Lace Market from a run down and depressing district, seemingly without a future, into an area of great diversity and interest.

Buildings which stood empty and unused for many years have been refurbished; landscaped sites have matured into attractive oases of green and there are residents back in the heart of the city for the first time in many years. Although much remains to be done, a great deal has been achieved as a result of a decade of effort by the City Planning Depart-

58

26: Halifax Place — blending in the Lace Market's first new housing for 100 years.

ment. This was recognised in 1983 with the award of the RTPI Jubilee Silver Cup for Planning Achievement and a Europa Nostra award in the same year.

It took architects of the calibre of Hine and Fothergill to give the Lace market its distinctive face. Less well known were the Booker family, an architectural partnership with offices on Short Hill. William, Frederick and Robert (William's son) were founder members of the Nottingham Architectural Association, later affiliated to the Royal Institute of British Architects. After changes in title, it continues today as the East Midlands Region of the RIBA. Appropriately a new generation of architects, planners and developers are now forging ahead with an exciting and enterprising series of projects to give the area a vibrant new lease of life.

Tenants are moving into the ground floor of the six-storey Victorian

27: Sharespace Two in a building formerly occupied by Stiebel.

lace warehouse on the corner of Stoney Street and Plumtre Street. Sharespace Two follows the original Sharespace complex at King John's Chambers, off Bridlesmith Gate. It will house 40 independent companies, whose business is communication,especially in print. They will include business start-ups, small firms and more established, larger companies.

The handsome building, overlooking St Mary's Church, was formerly occupied by Stiebel before they moved to new premises at Lenton industrial estate. It was bought by Bob Marshall, of Marshall Sutton (Notts) Ltd, for £65,000 two years ago and about £300,000 is being spent on internal and external refurbishments.

The first tenant is Nottinghamshire Chamber of Commerce, moving the training premises for its much-praised Youth Training Scheme into the ground floor. The 600 places on the present scheme are expected to expand during the next year and the new premises in the Lace Market are seen as an ideal, central location.

At the other end of the business spectrum are two penthouse offices — formerly a lace designing studio — offering prestigious accommodation of unusual character with unrivalled views around the city. Although strictly not for clock watchers, the suite looks out directly on to the clock face of St Mary's Church and offers panoramic views of Nottingham, including the Castle, Central TV's new studios and Player's Horizon factory.

Sharespace director Andrew James says: "The structure of the building was very sound but we are completely renovating it internally. Heating, electricity and plumbing were taken out so that we were left with a shell and we have now replaced all those services."

The development project, by Marshall James, is let and managed by Andrew James. The aim is to provide working spaces where firms can grow as their business develops and benefit from contact with others in related businesses. Back up support for the tenants includes telephone manning, typing, book keeping and VAT services, word processing, photocopying and free business advice from Action Resource Centre.

Equally challenging is a proposed new visitor's centre in the Lace Market area to help develop Nottingham's great tourist potential. The city has made tremendous strides in this direction and with the creation of the Royal Centre has soon established itself as a major conference centre.

The Lace Market Centre will serve several purposes, showing off the city's rich heritage to visitors, both tourists and businessmen, and provide an interesting showcase to promote industry, commerce and the city itself. It will house a wide variety of facilities such as permanent displays, exhibition space, an audio-visual auditorium and conference rooms. Therewill also be a retail sales area and a cafe-restaurant.

As a first step, the City Council bought for just over £50,000 the former High Pavement Chapel, with its splendid collection of stained glass, which will make a magnificent backdrop to the new activities now proposed.

The lavish chapel, which cost £12,000, opened in April, 1876. It was clearly intended to rival St Mary's, the parish church of Nottingham further up High Pavement which is one of the finest examples of the

61

28: High Pavement Chapel.

29: The magnificent stained glass windows in the chancel.

30: An impression of the Lace Market Centre.

perpendicular style in the country. Papers show how instructions were given to erect a spire 10ft higher than St Mary's tower. Despite surviving first the onslaught of the railway age 20 years later when a new line scythed through the city centre and then one of the few bombing raids on Nottingham which left gaps in the Lace Market, the Unitarian chapel failed to escape problems of post-war dwindling congregations. The chapel is now listed, with the most precious and valuable aspects, the memorial window in the chancel, valued by top London fine art dealers at £100,000. Designed by the leading Anglican pre-Raphaelite Edward Burne-Jones and executed by Morris and Co, they depict images of late Victorian chivalry and standards. An imaginative scheme has been drawn up and the Government-backed Inner Area Programme and the Historic Buildings Council is willing to contribute financially towards the conversion. The response from the private sector has been encouraging too. So it is hoped to form a partnership effort to promote Nottingham, Queen of the Midlands. Certainly it is a project which deserves to succeed.

The excellent new fashion centre on the ground floor of the Price building at 37 Stoney Street also promises to be a marvellous shot in the arm for the city's clothing and textile industries. Under its director Susan Spencer, it will provide centralised marketing and business assistance and in the applications of new technology will work very closely with the Advanced Business Centre, also being pioneered by the City Council.

The centre will have almost continuous exhibitions of fashion products, probably organised by themes. Lace, jewellery (related to fashion), shoes and other accessories will also be featured in addition to clothing and textiles. The architect and interior designer for the project is Peter Hill of Cullen, Carter and Hill. a Nottingham firm with considerable experience in working on buildings in the Lace Market.

Of the 6,000 sq ft within the Fashion Centre, 4,500 sq ft will be devoted to flexible exhibition space, within which there will a 100-seat auditorium and stage which will be used for training lectures, business seminars and, of course, fashion shows.

There will be a conference room — the refurbished original conference room in the Price building — offices, a small library, reception area, bar and kitchen.

Most of the renovation and modernisation has been carried out by the owners of the building and the City Council is spending £80,000 for the fixtures and fitting and other capital costs.

As a focal point to promote local industry, the Fashion Centre will have several functions. In addition to fashion exhibitions and displays it will provide back up and general assistance in marketing and product design.

Meanwhile urban development grants are changing the face of Nottingham. Schemes, which by themselves are not commercially viable, became possible when aided by Government and local authority contributions. The aim is to encourage investment and bring about physical and economic regeneration, not only in inner city areas but in urban areas generally. The scheme, based on a successful American concept — the US Urban Development Action Grant — has been taken up with enthusiasm in Nottingham, which, in the first year, did rather better than any other city in terms of both number of grants awarded and financial value.

One of the five schemes given the go-ahead was a £1.57m project to convert the disused former Lambert's factory in Talbot Street, a listed building, into an 80-bedroom hotel. Elsewhere around the city it's easy to find sites worthy of similar treatment.

For within the inner city area and beyond, a high number of large, old industrial buildings, vacant or under occupied, require major investment to bring them back into full use. Sadly some are beyond recall — vandals, for example, gutted an empty factory on Beech Avenue. Fire is another arch enemy as witnessed by the massive blaze which gutted Swiss Mills, Beeston. It represented a link betwen lace manufacture in this country and the United States because in 1900 ambitious plans were made to start a lace factory in Zion City, near Chicago. Samuel Stevenson, operating at that time in Swiss Mills, became a Zionist and arranged to bring machinery and workers from Beeston. The factory in Villa Street, forming the rear end of Swiss Mills, was one of the oldest lace factories in the district and was probably erected during the 1820s or 30s when lace and bobbin net was spreading westwards from Nottingham. It was used in the 1860s by William Felkin junior, son of the lace and hosiery historian who also had a lace factory in Beeston.

65

31: The burned-out shell of the Swiss Mills, Beeston.

The sale of one of the oldest lace factories in the city on Mansfield Road could also mark the end of an era. The imposing four storey building, which is not listed, interested industrial conservationists because the rear dates from around 1825 and the front from about 1880.

Meanwhile Stuart Warburton and Ian Todd performed a very valuable and useful survey, spending a year recording as much of Nottingham's industrial heritage as they could, as part of a community programme.

Stuart says: "Nottingham is really rich in interesting buildings and by and large has a good record in conservation. But it has a lot to preserve and you cannot save everything. So some buildings may have to be sacrificed for others."

One property he would certainly like to be listed is 117 North Gate in New Basford because it is possibly the only surviving portion of development from the 1820s when the district started to absorb some of Nottingham's industrial overspill.

Another gem is the weaver's cottage on Alfreton Road, next door to the Alma Inn. Built around 1823 and exceptionally well preserved, it's "top shop" attic suggests it was used by a framework knitter or as a domestic lace workshop.

The planners have chalked up some notable successes in the industrial improvement and general improvement areas. But Stuart and Ian believe there is ample scope for Nottingham starting one or several industrial trails. And an indication of the level of interest came when the Planning Department produced a Lace Market Trail. There was a strong demand for leaflets, which help visitors understand and appreciate one of England's most interesting industrial quarters.

Incidentally if you are browsing around the buildings of the Lace Market, there's much to admire in St Mary's Church, including a memorial to Thomas Adams and a Leavers lace machine. On certain days you can even engage in a spot of brass rubbing.

The survival and revival of the Lace Market now seems assured. Many visitors ask if it's possible to tour lace finishing firms in the district and perhaps this is a facility one or two manufacturers could explore by organising the occasional open day.

Improvement Area status for the Lace Market expired in May, 1984. What happens next depends to some extent on the local authority and the private sector. But mostly it's also up to us.

CHAPTER NINE
New Trends, Old Trends

Hand made lace is coming into its own again. Indeed the Jewel, the insignia of office worn by the President of the British Lace Federation, which appears on our front cover, is a gold and enamel reproduction of an old lady making pillow lace. Even within the lace manufacturing industry there is now a new consciousness of the beauty and craftsmanship of old pieces, coupled with a remarkable revival in bobbin lacemaking.

Thousands of women are attending classes, twisting threads to make intricate and exquisite patterns. The art appeals to all age groups, schoolgirls, teenagers, young mums, middle aged women as well as the older generation.

The Nottinghamshire Bobbin Lace Society has grown to over 400 members and about 20 classes, run in most parts of the county, are usually fully booked. Mrs Ann Seals, who teaches the craft to City and Guilds examination level at West Notts College, Mansfield, says: "Bobbin lace is now an accepted part of the creative textiles course. There is tremendous interest in the whole range of hand made laces, traditional and modern. Marvellous lacemakers like Ann Collier of London are taking the art into new directions, developing techniques and styles so that the finished piece takes the form of a picture."

The favourite item in Ann Seal's own portfolio is a Floral Bucks point ground collar, which required over 70 pairs of bobbins and took two and a half years to make. "I now need the right dress to take the collar," she says with a smile.

It's a craft that calls for the utmost care and patience. Before starting a pricking, Ann draughts the design on paper and will make minor modifications as the work progresses.

Ann has hundreds of bobbins and many are made by Dennis Thornton, who operates from a little workshop in Trinity Square, Nottingham. The business, H. and T. Bobbin Company, began almost by accident and with rudimentary equipment. Now Dennis supplies many of the lace

68

circles, some large stores and exports to enthusiasts abroad. "The bobbins are so well finished," says Ann.

Bobbin lace is almost exclusively a feminine hobby. So Bob Coombs must be one of Britain's only male bobbin lacemakers. An electronics lecturer at Broxtowe College, he decided to join Mary Gregory's class last September and took to the pins like a natural.

He's already had two pieces in exhibitions and is currently working on a Continental lace collar, which is stretching his skills to the utmost with 40 pairs of bobbins in use in some sections.

Bob says: "I find it quite relaxing because it's totally different from my job." He moved from the North East to the Top Valley area of the city, where his wife is warden of an old people's home. A man of many talents, he also enjoys knitting, embroidery, crochet and marquetry and for good measure has started collecting bobbins in the hope of acquiring some antiques ones, which are growing in value.

Is bobbin lace about to turn full circle? After all, it started as a cottage industry, involving wives and children, as a way of supplementing the farm wages of their menfolk. When the machine age arrived, men assumed the key role of twisthands, forming an aristocracy among local workers with many taverns having a room reserved "for twisthands only."

Ann Seals, who regularly gives bobbin lace demonstrations at Nottingham Lace Centre, says the centuries-old craft is always creating something new. For example, hand made lace fans are coming back into fashion and one of Ann's students in another college group, Wendy Bush, is busy completing a set of fingerless mittens to wear at her wedding. Ann says: "They have been designed so that Wendy has no trouble getting the ring on her finger! It should complete her wedding outfit since her dress incorporates machine made lace.I think hand and machine lace are quite compatible."

But how is Nottingham's famous lace industry fairing at present? You could say it's in the pink. For two-tone tights in pink, or platinum and white, are attracting international orders for a Langley Mill hosiery firm. Since Aristoc launched their new range, the French have gone dotty about spots while the Americans are falling for Nottingham lace tights in a big way.

It is, says fashion co-ordinator Hilary Barrett, evidence that fashion is going to women's legs and sales executive Barry Surtees is enthusiastic about the latest range, which includes knee and ankle socks as well as tights. "I am absolutely delighted to be selling a locally made product that has the name of Nottingham associated with it," he said. Multi-coloured mini spots are aimed at the young while white lace tights are selling well to spring brides.

On a broader front what is the state of the lace trade generally? The industry has seen an upturn during the last 18 months. Last year was very good and 1984 started off equally well. "Obviously you get ups and downs with different sorts of things, but by and large trade is very good indeed," says Ronald Walton, Director of the British Lace Federation.

32: Ann Seals at work on a piece of pillow lace.

33: Three examples of Ann Seal's work, including a Floral Bucks point ground collar, which required over 70 pairs of bobbins.

The industry has been through a fairly long period of consolidation with amalgamations and other changes, he says. There are now a smallish number of firms, but they are successful. New technology has been adopted for the high speed Raschel machines with some remarkable developments during the last ten years. Firms like Fletchers of Heanor, who in the main produce dress type laces, are at the head of the field.

The Princess of Wales has brought a lace look to fashion which has done the lace trade no harm at all. New trends are forever finding their way into an old industry, which abounds with characters, some retired, some still hard at work.

Charles Lawson, believed to be Britain's oldest sales representative, prefers an early start. He's often up at the crack of dawn to be on the road to Birmingham before the morning rush hour begins. He's turned 80 but could easily be mistaken for 60. "I have no intention of retiring," he says. "I like meeting people and getting out and about. I really enjoy work."

Charles, who lives in the Aspley district of Nottingham, began his career in the lace trade at 14 working at Flersheim's lace warehouse in St Mary's Gate. He recalls: "I worked like a little galley slave, carrying great pieces of plain net up five flights of stairs and operating a huge guillotine. I earned 5s a week which all went to my mother, who gave me 6d a week back for spending money." The hours were 9am till 6 or 7pm at night. On Saturday afternoon he remembers anxiously watching the clock as the minutes ticked away, eager to be off to the Forest match with his workmates. The office manager Mr Robinson would eye him severely and say: "So you think more about football than the firm. Come on lad, get those last orders finished before you leave."

Those were the days when lace and the lacemasters ruled. Charles remembers seeing hundreds of lace girls streaming out of the Stoney Street factories at Saturday lunchtime. During the dark days of war, he also recalls a Heinkel flying overhead, spattering bullets along the pavement, perilously close to where he was walking.

He later established himself as a traveller for the firm, opening up many new outlets in Ireland and South Wales. Often he spent six weeks at a time in Ireland, travelling far and wide. He particularly enjoyed staying in the comfortable hotels of Dublin and getting to know his customers in that fair city. "They were happy times," he recalls.

Charles vividly remembers one mouth-watering meal just after the Second World War. "The Irish waiter brought in the biggest plate of meat I'd ever seen. After rationing, it seemed like a feast."

Business began to pick up again. But sadly Flersheim's went into liquidation in 1969. Charles had worked for the firm for 46 years and it was six months before the Redundancy Act was passed. So there was no compensation or pension. "I had to do something," says Charles. He became an agent for two companies and today keeps busy travelling throughout the Midlands. Charles proudly showed me his case containing lace samples. One of the exclusive lines he sells, a beautiful macrame chairback cover, graces the restaurant cars of the world's most famous train — the Orient Express.

72

34: Lace tights by Aristoc in a subtly sophisticated pattern.

Charles likes to travel. By bicycle and car he's covered almost the entire coastline of the British Isles — apart from the Limerick-Galway stretch in Southern Ireland. "It's my ambition to do that one day," he says. And he has loved every minute of holidays in Spain and elsewhere with his daughter Jane and her family. Jane, who now lives in London, says: "He's a fantastic person. In Spain he was galloping around with the children."

Charles, a widower, who has two grandchildren, says: "I have been very lucky. I have a very good family, some marvellous friends and wonderful neighbours." He is also a long-serving governor at St Teresa's School and an active member of the church near his home in Kingsbury Drive. "Saturday morning I usually spend cleaning and washing but if I have a few minutes I go visiting the old folk in the parish," he says with a smile. In 1960 he was presented with the Papal medal "Pro Ecclesia et Pontifice" in recognition of his diocesan work for Catholic education.

Long may this charming character continue to represent the lace industry and his community so well.

CHAPTER TEN

Lace in the Computer Age

Directors of the Birkin Group take great pride in the seal and scroll hanging in the reception area of their Nottingham headquarters. Dated 1857, it gave Birkin and Co Ltd., the patent rights to produce figured laces. And in those days, that seal was backed by the might of the British Empire, gunboats and all!

This is a company steeped in history. Established in 1827 by Richard Birkin, one of the pioneers of the trade, it is the oldest Leavers lace manufacturing firm in the world. Yet no one can accuse Birkins of basking in old glories. The group, was formed in 1961-2 by the merger of four family firms — Birkin and Co. Ltd., Arthur Tunnicliffe and Son Ltd., J. Guy and Co. Ltd., and J. Fearfield Ltd. This brought together formidable production and marketing resources. Today the group — one of the world leaders of the lace industry — exports to more than 20 countries and is at the forefront of the latest technology.

In 1983 they installed a £100,000 computer-operated machine — the first of its kind in the world. The new Jacquardtronic system, operating at the company's Knitted Lace Division at Borrowash, near Derby, put Birkin's ahead of all its competitors, including those in America and Japan. It was developed in close association with Karl Mayer, the German textile machine builders.

David Attenborough, Birkin's managing director and chief executive, said: "This is the most advanced lacemaking system in the world. We now have three of the machines operating, producing high quality laces, which are in strong demand from our customers. Our order books are full until autumn and an Australian firm has placed a big repeat order. The equipment is computer operated and includes a new pattern control system which enables rapid design changes to be made.

"However, the really exciting breakthrough is our ability to emulate fine gauge clipped Leavers lace, previously only available in France at very high prices. While the textile industry has been going through its worst recession in memory, we are convinced there is a future for the specialist producer, capable of using the tremendous advances in technology now available."

75

35. Barry Stocks, director in charge of Birkin's Knitted Lace Division with the Jacquardtronic machine.

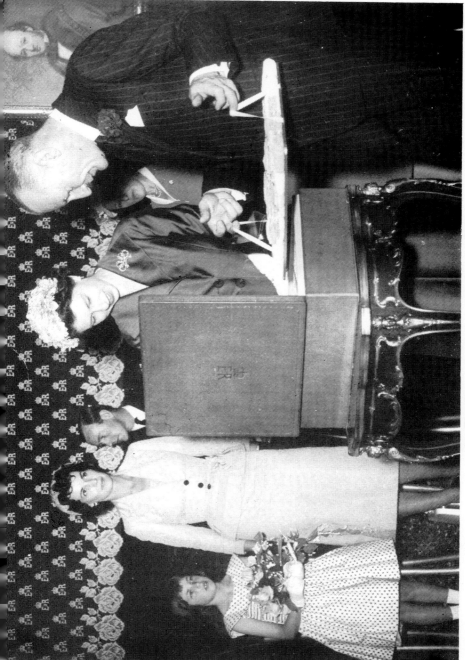

36: The Queen's visit to Birkins in 1955.

Development work for the new machine was carried out in Obsertshausen in West Germany, and in Fukui, Japan.

Mr Barry Stocks, director in charge of Birkin's Raschel Division, said: "We can now change a pattern in under two hours, compared with about a week on existing machines. The new system, will also produce lace at a far greater speed than the latest Japanese machine — 25 per cent faster. With the help of the computer and the new Jacquard technology, we can now make far more complex and beautiful laces than on existing Raschel machinery.

"Using the new system in conjunction with our automatic clipping machines, the only one of its kind in this country, we can reproduce old Edwardian and Victorian patterns which have not been produced here for many years."

The pattern bars on the Jacquardtronic machine are operated electronically by computer, controlled by using a magnetic tape. This process eliminates the need for thousands of chain links which previously had to be hand-assembled into a pattern chain. This is a dirty, laborious job which can take up to two weeks.

Corrections and alterations to new patterns can also be done through the use of the computer's visual display unit and keyboard, in a fraction of the time taken previously.

And later this year the company takes delivery of another machine — again the first of its kind in the world — which will have even greater design capacity.

Yet it has taken a massive amount of teamwork and faith in the company's abilities to achieve its present position of strength.

At the end of 1979 the recession meant that Birkin's went from substantial profit to report losses for the first time and within six months the company was forced to cut its workforce from 430 to 260.

Exports to its most lucrative market, Japan, plummeted, caused by a worldwide fall in demand, cost inflation and the high level of sterling, which put Britain in a weak exporting position.

But the lace trade is accustomed to slumps as well as peaks in it's history, usually due to changes in fashion. With all the inherited experience, it knows not only how to ride the storm but lay the foundations of future prosperity.

And so it was with Birkins. The character and commitment of their entire workforce ensured survival and the company emerged from this traumatic period better equipped to face the challenge of the 80s. They pushed ahead with major development on a vacant factory site at Borrowash. This was virtually demolished and re-built before advanced plant could be transferred from Draycott, including the installation of eight Mayer 42 and 52-bar machines — the only ones of their type operating in the UK.

The oldest Leavers lace manufacturers now has the most modern, knitted lace factory in the world. Advanced air-conditioning plant controls the temperature to within one degree and the same equipment also controls the humidity — all necessary to produce the best running conditions for the sophisticated machinery. The humidity control also cuts out all static electricity produced by the combination of synthetic yarns and fast running machinery.

The factory has its own generator that cuts in automatically in the case of an electricity failure. A further security is the boiler plant, which can be operated on either gas or oil at the flick of a switch. This has 12 small boilers instead of one large one so that in the event of a breakdown only 1/12th of heating capacity would be lost and the effect on output reduced to a minimum.

The 1979 lace machinery exhibition in Hanover proved to be a significant turning point for the trade. Raschel machines, producing knitted laces at high speed, first appeared in 1952. At first patterns were very simple but gradually techniques improved, bringing down the cost relative to other textiles, particularly embroidery.

Every few years the leading lace machine manufacturer brought out a machine with more pattern bars. Then in 1979 a bombshell hit the trade. A competitor had ideas on the drawing board for a computerised machine with unrivalled design capacity. Karl Mayer, responded to the threat by seeking precise specifications from Birkins, a giant American company and a major West German lace manufacturer to determine their exact needs for the next generation of lace machinery. The result was the Jacquardtronic, a marvellous success story. Something of a race developed between Birkins and their West German rivals to be first to go into production. Birkins won.

Since then the company has gone from strength to strength. Sales have increased ten times since the group was formed. They won major orders in Australia, extended their business in America and Japan, achieved excellent sales in South Africa and Europe, particularly Germany and broke into the exclusive French market which is the equivalent of "selling coals to Newcastle." In 1983 sales were 20 per cent higher than expected with new orders up by 30 per cent over budget. And 1984 shaped up as another excellent year.

The Borrowash factory is on a six-and-a-half day week round-the-clock working, with its 30 machines in full capacity. The 40 Leavers machines at their two Long Eaton factories are also kept busy and the demand for lace was so great that some employees at the Nottingham factory gave up part of their holidays to finish a 230,000 metre order. Incidentally at Birkins it's best to think of lace in miles rather than metres. One machine alone at the Borrowash factory can turn out 70 miles of lace a week.

David Attenborough said: "We are delighted to be receiving orders at a very high level and this has largely been achieved by designing exactly the type of lace which is being demanded by buyers and the public. The emphasis has changed from trying to sell designs which we think people will want, to selling women the kind of lace they are asking for. The result is that we have been much more successful than we ever imagined with sales and orders at a very satisfactory level."

A profit-sharing scheme has been introduced so that all the company's

79

37: Alan Moore, chief draughtsman and Carol Deboo, digitiser, using the computer aided equipment for draughting knitted lace.

38: Tasteful use of lace on modern intimate apparel.

336 employees can benefit from their "terrific" efforts. Chairman Mr Walter Tunnicliffe and his board are also big believers in good communication at all levels of the company.

Every month 15-strong groups of workers attend brief-in sessions, led by their departmental heads, to talk about the latest developments in the firm, discuss progress and possible improvements. The firm also puts a strong emphasis on training.

Ninety per cent of Birkin's production goes on garments, the vast majority of it appearing on intimate apparel — briefs, bras, lingerie, nightwear and girdles. Marks and Spencer and other leading UK brand houses are among the firm's major customers. During the past 20 years Birkin's technicians have developed many exciting new ideas, including an additional dimension in the form of stretch, which has enabled customers to incorporate lace into a whole new range of garments. At their works in New Basford, lace is put through a comprehensive series of tests. They even have a device to check the bursting strength of a bra.

More and more the emphasis is on superb quality and design. And the latest technology is opening up exciting possibilities for new products and patterns, previously considered too intricate.

The capacity of the Jacquardtronic is so great that one customer was able to see a draft sample within a week of choosing a design. Computers have taken a lot of the drudgery out of lace draughting. But the skill and artistry of designers and draughtsmen is as great as ever. It is often said there is no design which has not already been produced at some time during the long history of lace making. And Birkins, with a marvellous library of many thousands of designs produced over 150 years, should know. Yet during the last 20 years their designers and draughtsmen have created more than 3,000 new designs.

Barry Stocks loves looking at the old pattern books, containing exquisite and remarkable designs such as the one produced in 1855 for Wimbledon, showing tennis rackets with the strings etched in red.

Barry says: "The new technology is opening up many exciting possibilities for the future. In one sense we have only just started to scratch the surface. The potential is immense and we have many ideas we want to try."

That enthusiasm is shared by David Attenborough, who says: "I love the lace business. It has brought me a few headaches over the years, but a great sense of achievement too."

Although he now holds a position of respect and influence, he has not forgotten humbler, younger days when he had to start at the bottom, doing menial jobs like sweeping the factory floor, as the third generation of his family in the firm of J. Fearfield Ltd. Neither has he forgotten that firms are most of all about people.

He has a sense of history too. He was sad when vandals gutted an empty factory across the road from Birkin's Beech Avenue Works, which houses the group's sales departments, central services, finishing, processing, shipping and despatch and the firm's computers. The Maville Works have been given an £18,000 facelift as part of the New Basford industrial improvement scheme.

Proudly taking the visitor on a whistle-stop tour of the works, he points to the area where a bank of VDU's will soon absorb masses of the firm's paperwork.

So how does the boss of one of the most go-ahead firms see the future of the lace trade in a computer age? David Attenborough accepts that only companies of a certain size will be able to afford the new generation of computerised lace making machinery. Five years ago the most advanced 52-bar Raschel machine cost £50,000. Now the most sophisticated technology will cost three or four times that amount. But he believes that efficient firms can still survive and prosper.

Picture Credits

Photographs and illustrations used in this book were from a number of sources. Every endeavour has been made to obtain authority to use copyright material but apology is offered to any whose right may have been inadvertantly infringed. Thanks are expressed to the following:

Plate 1: Nottinghamshire Local Studies Library.
Plate 2: Nottingham Evening Post.
Plate 3: Reg Packer.
Plate 4: Nottinghamshire Local Studies Library.
Plate 5: Nottingham Evening Post.
Plate 6: Nottingham Evening Post.
Plate 7: Nottingham Evening Post.
Plate 8: Nottingham Evening Post.
Plate 9: A. C. Gill.
Plate 10: A. C. Gill.
Plate 11: Supplied.
Plate 12: Hawaii Visitor's Centre.
Plate 13: Sheraton Hotels and Inns Worldwide.
Plate 14: Nottingham Evening Post.
Plate 15: Nottingham Evening Post.
Plate 16: Nottingham Evening Post.
Plate 17: Lace Research Association.
Plate 18: Lace Research Association.
Plate 19: Layland Ross Ltd.
Plate 20: Nottingham Evening Post.
Plate 21: Nottingham Evening Post.
Plate 22: Lace Research Association.
Plate 23: Supplied.
Plate 24: Edgar Lloyd.
Plate 25: Jim Bancroft.
Plate 26: John Critchley.
Plate 27: Andrew James.
Plate 28: Nottingham Evening Post.
Plate 29: Nottingham Evening Post.
Plate 30: Nottingham Planning Department.
Plate 31: Nottingham Evening Post.
Plate 32: Nottingham Evening Post.
Plate 33: Nottingham Evening Post.
Plate 34: Aristoc.
Plate 35: Raymonds, Derby.
Plate 36: Supplied.
Plate 37: Raymonds, Derby.
Plate 38: Murray Irving.
Back cover photograph of Jacquardtronic: Raymonds, Derby.

Lace Collections

For those wishing to delve deeper, we thought it useful to mention museums and centres in Nottingham, Britain and abroad holding lace collections and exhibits of special interest. This is in no sense an exhaustive list.

NOTTINGHAMSHIRE.

The Museum of Costume and Textiles:
An elegant row of Georgian terrace houses, built 1788, containing the city's costume, lace and textile collections. Includes a series of six period rooms containing costume from about 1750 to about 1960. Open: All year daily 10-5. Closed on Christmas Day. Admission free. Enquiries to 43-51 Castlegate, Nottingham. Tel. (0602) 411881.

Industrial Museum, Wollaton Park:
Displays in 18th century stable block — about three miles from the city — presenting a history of Nottingham industries, including lace. Superb collection of machines and other exhibits on view. Open: April to September, Monday to Saturday 10-6; Sunday 2-6. October to March, Thursday and Saturday 10-4.30; Sunday 1.30-4.30. Closed on Christmas Day. Admission free. (Sundays and Bank holidays 15p). Enquiries to Courtyard Buildings, Wollaton Park, Nottingham. Tel. (0602) 284602.

The Lace Centre:
Within a stone's throw of the Castle Gatehouse (and almost opposite the Robin Hood statue), stands a reconstructed 15th century timber-framed building known as Severns, once a well known restaurant on the edge of the Lace Market. The centre contains displays telling the story of lace from medieval times to present day and there is a superb collection of Nottingham lace for sale. Also on view, some traditional bobbin lace, interesting exhibits and a miniature lace machine. Open: Daily 10-5, apart from mid-winter when it opens 11-4. Admission free. Enquiries to Nottingham Lace Centre Ltd., Severns Building, Castle Road, Nottingham. Tel (0602) 413539.

Calverton Museum:
Beautifully restored cottage in Main Street, Calverton, a village about six miles from Nottingham. Dedicated to the memory of the Rev William Lee, the kitchen looks as it would have done when the house was built in 1780. There is an Edwardian style bedroom as well as interesting exhibits, including a hand frame knitting machine. Open: By appointment. Further details from Mrs Eileen Cupitt, secretary of the Calverton Preservation Society, 142 Main Street, Calverton. Tel. (0602) 652836.

Ruddington Framework Knitters' Museum:
Volunteers have put years of effort into this enterprising project for industrial heritage at Chapel Street, Ruddington — about five miles from Nottingham. A restored frame shop puts visitors straight back into the 19th century when framework knitting was an important industry in Ruddington. Eleven hand frames are in operation. Courses run for those interested in learning how to use a hand frame — instruction available. An exciting exhibition room and lecture theatre opened in May, 1982 and a second exhibition room opened in September, 1983 covering the local aspects of hand frame knitting. Open: By appointment. Special open days arranged during the summer. Further details from Mrs J. R. Beardall, Long Acre, Old Road, Ruddington. Tel (0602) 213287 or Mrs J. B. Coates, 34 Musters Road, Ruddington. Tel (0602) 211858.

London: The Victoria and Albert Museum.

Luton: Superb collection of handmade lace. Further information from Mrs Fudge, curator of the Lace Department. Luton Museum and Art Gallery, Wardown Park, Luton, Beds., LU2 7HA.

Bedford: Interesting exhibits at Bedford Museum in Castle Lane and fine collection of lace, including Thomas Lester designs at the nearby Cecil Higgins Art Gallery in Castle Close.

Rockbeare, near Exeter, Devon: The English Lace School. Founded in 1979 to provide a centre for the study of lace in this country, it welcomes complete beginners as well as experienced lacemakers. They run special classes for adults and children and organise international festivals of lace. Further information from Mrs Susan Cox, Principal, The English Lace School, Honiton Court, Rockbeare, near Exeter, EX5 2EF. Tel (0404) 822735.

Exeter: The Royal Albert Memorial Museum. Permanent displays of Honiton and other lace. Large reserve collections, including Bury Palliser and Treadwin collections can be seen by prior arrangement. Open: 10-5.15 Tuesday to Saturday. Further information from the Museum, Queen Street, Exeter. Tel (0392) 56724.

Interesting centres abroad include the Irle-Jacoby Collection at St. Gall, Switzerland and museums in Bruges, Bayeaux and Amsterdam.